Worshiping God with Our Children
Edith Bajema

A FAMILY AFFAIR

CRC Publications
Grand Rapids, Michigan

Acknowledgments

Edith Bajema, author of *A Family Affair: Worshiping God with Our Children*, is a free-lance writer and editor living in Grand Rapids, Michigan. She has been very active in involving the children of her congregation in worship.

The Scripture quotations in this publication are from the HOLY BIBLE, NEW INTERNATIONAL VERSION, copyright © 1973, 1978, 1984, International Bible Society. Used by permission of Zondervan Bible publishers.

A Family Affair
Worshiping God with our Children

Originally printed in 1990 under the title *Worship: Not for Adults Only.* Copyright © 1990, 1994 by CRC Publications, 2850 Kalamazoo SE, Grand Rapids, Michigan 4960.

Library of Congress Cataloging-in-Publication Data
Bajema, Edith, 1952-
   [Worship, not for adults only]
   A family affair: worshiping God with our children / Edith Bajema.
      p.   cm. — (Issues in Christian living)
   Originally published under title: Worship, not for adults only. 1990.
   Includes bibliographical references.
   ISBN 1-56212-063-8: $6.50
   1. Children in public worship—Reformed Church. 2. Worship (Religious education) 3. Family—Religious life. 4. Children—Religious life. I. Title. II. Series.
[BV26.2.B33   1994]
249—dc20
                                       94-3460
                                           CIP

10 9 8 7 6 5 4 3 2

C O N T E N T S

INTRODUCTION 5
SESSION 1: WHAT IS WORSHIP? 9
SESSION 2: A CHILD'S VIEW 21
SESSION 3: A HISTORICAL PERSPECTIVE 35
SESSION 4: WORSHIPING TOGETHER AT HOME 49
SESSION 5: WORSHIPING TOGETHER AT CHURCH 65
SESSION 6: THE WORSHIP CONNECTION 81
RESOURCES 95

INTRODUCTION

T his course invites you to reflect on the meaning of worship for you and for the children you know and love. Worship is at the very heart of the kingdom. In fact, worship is one place in this fractured world where old and young can come together to create something that resembles the kingdom of heaven.

In this course we encourage you, with the members of your group, to look at worship in a new way, with the eyes of a child. Explore together the disturbing and refreshing message of Jesus' words: "I tell you the truth, unless you change and become like little children you will never enter the kingdom of heaven."

The Abba sat under the shade of his tree one day, patiently listening to the voice of the wind above him. There came to him a young man, well-dressed, with a certain expression on his face that the Abba had learned to recognize as self-satisfaction.

"Abba," said the young man, "I am seeking for God. I have heard that you know many things about God, I would like you to teach me how to know and worship him."

The Abba studied the face of the young man before him. Finally he said, "I will teach you. Come with me to the river."

So the Abba and the young man walked together in silence to the river. When they got there, the Abba stepped into the water and beckoned to the young man to follow him. They walked out until the water was above their waists.

"Now," said the Abba. "What is it that you want?"

"O great Abba, who is wise beyond many, I want to know and worship God," said the young man in his most pleasant and humble voice.

The Abba pushed the young man under the water and held him there for twenty seconds. Then he lifted the youth, sputtering, from the water. "What is it that you want?" he asked him again.

"Please, most honored Teacher, I wish you to teach me how I can know and worship God," said the young man.

The Abba again pushed the young man under the water, this time holding him there for more than thirty seconds. When he let the young man come up, he asked him again, "What is it that you want from me?"

Choking with water, the young man began, "I want, O Great One, to know—"

Immediately the Abba pushed him down under the water, holding him there firmly for almost a minute. The young man came up, wild-eyed and thrashing, shouting, "Air! Air! Give me air to breathe!"

The Abba waited until the youth had quieted down. Then he said to him, "When you desire to know and worship God with the same intensity as you desire air, you will find him."

This is a lovely story. The Abba—as people called the hermits and holy men who lived alone in the desert—spent his life meditating on the truths of God. Many people sought him out for spiritual guidance. "Abba," they said, "Open our eyes—show us how to live."

But what does this story have to do with a course for adults on children and worship?

Perhaps it has to do with keeping our eyes open. Perhaps it has to do with reexamining our assumptions about worship and about ourselves.

This is a course for adults. We will sit back in our chairs, get our notepads out, take pen in hand, and get ready to learn how to help our children do something that we already know how to do—worship.

But do we know how to worship?

Of course we do. How many worship services have we sat through since our childhood? Some of us may not have grown up attending church regularly; but many of us have. Every Sunday finds us in church. Some of us will have attended almost 4,000 worship services by the time we reach middle age. Churchgoing is part of our blood. If anyone knows how to worship, we do.

Or do we?

Perhaps before we talk about children and worship, the Abba would have us ask ourselves a few questions. What makes a worship service a *worship* service? What happens during that time that makes it worship? Do the forms and rituals themselves constitute worship? What is worship, at its essence?

The young man told the Abba that he desired to know and worship God. When we step into church on Sunday morning, in essence we are saying the same thing: we want to know and worship God. But our words, like the young man's, do not always ring true. The Abba calls us to question our assumptions. Do we desire to know and worship God? Does our worship reflect that longing?

The premise of this course is that to know and worship God is the deepest desire of the human spirit. It is the reason God created us. We exist in order to worship God, to respond to God's passion for us. The Scriptures tell us that God yearns for us, that his heart is charged with love and longing for us. God is passionate; he would give his own life to draw us to himself. Worship is our response to God's approach, an opening of ourselves to God. To know and worship God is the heart of the kingdom. From our worship of God flows all that we call "kingdom living."

This desire to know and worship God is as vital to children as it is to adults. And it may lie even closer to the surface in children, who tend to be much more direct than their elders. "Where is God, Mommy?" "How do I know God is in my heart? Why can't I feel him?" "Isn't God really everywhere?" "How come we go to church to worship him?"

Children don't beat around the bush when talking about God. They are curious about the words that adults use, especially words that describe the greatest of all mysteries: knowing God.

We all shared this curiosity and directness as children. But something happened to words like "worship" and "God" and "believe" as we got older. These words were once sharp with meaning and with mystery. They intrigued us, poked at us, made us ask questions. But now they roll off our tongues like pebbles worn smooth with years of use. We don't feel their sharp edges. We assume that we know their meaning, and they no longer disturb us.

Do we know the meaning of worship? Perhaps the first thing we need to do in this course, before we talk about the children, is to examine this question.

As we work our way through the issues related to children and worship, we will look at ways to teach our children about worshiping God, ways to involve them in family and public worship. But—in the arena of worship at least—we cannot lead our children where we do not go ourselves.

To view worship with a childlike freshness, we'll not use theological definitions. Instead, we'll begin this course by looking at our own experiences of worship—as children, as adolescents, as adults. What has worship meant to us at different times and in different places? How did our families worship? What are our earliest memories of church services? When have we felt the presence of God? What words or phrases would we use to describe these experiences?

If we aren't able to describe worship with words that flow from our own experience, our children may come to think worship is something we talk about, not something we do. And that would be as deadening for their worship as it is for ours.

WHAT IS WORSHIP?

This session will not seek to define worship. That task is left to you. This session will, however, raise some questions that will help you think. And discussing these questions with your group will broaden your appreciation for the richness of meaning and the wide variety of experiences that go into the word *worship*. Working with these questions will also help you to build a personal road map of your journey to know and worship God. Though your map will not be the same as anyone else's, you will find it useful in the rest of this course.

Feel free to disagree, to question, to challenge the assumptions made here. But however you respond to these thoughts and questions, make good use of the Bible and of your own experience to back up your challenges.

And tread lightly when you disagree with someone else in the group. Your discussion will touch on some of the deep places of the human spirit. Remember that God makes himself known to us in an infinite variety of ways; others may not meet God the way that you do. And you need not feel bound to meet God in the same way that others so confidently or enthusiastically describe.

What Does It Mean That God Is Present During Worship?

The old phrases and explanations roll readily off our tongues: "In worship we come before God's throne of grace"; "God is present through the Word and sacraments"; "the worship liturgy is a dialogue between God and his people."

We need to back off from these easy phrases and admit, first of all, that God's presence in worship is a mystery. As we sing in the communion hymn, "Gift of Finest Wheat,"

The mystery of your presence, Lord,
no mortal tongue can tell:
whom all the world cannot contain
comes in our hearts to dwell.

Our best attempts to describe God are but shadows of the truth. We say that God is present in his sanctuary, but none of us is completely sure what that means.

We confess that God is present through the Word that is read and preached. The Word is a sword that cuts into our hearts and minds. Sometimes we feel its sharpness and sense God's presence at work. Sometimes we don't.

We confess that God is present through the sacraments of baptism and Communion. We believe that something really happens here. In baptism, the relationship between the child and God shifts; something has changed. In communion, something changes in us when we eat and drink the body and blood of Christ; we believe that our spirits are nourished by this food. When we touch and taste the earthy symbols of water, bread, and wine, we are sometimes aware that we touch a great mystery—the presence of the invisible God.

We confess that God is present in the variety of gifts that are given to individuals in the congregation. Scripture gets quite specific here: "When you come together, everyone has a hymn, or a word of instruction, a revelation, a tongue or an interpretation" (1 Cor. 14:26). No one is left out of this: "Now to each one the manifestation of the Spirit is given for the common good" (12:7). Our tradition has not made much use of this way of involving people in worship. Nevertheless, the Bible is clear that the gifts used in worship include prophecy, the message of wisdom, the message of knowledge, the gift of faith, spiritual discernment, and so on—all of which apparently functioned regularly in New Testament worship. The Spirit makes itself known among us through the gifts it brings.

Yet though we can list some of the ways God is present—through the Word, sacraments, spiritual gifts—complete understanding of his presence is beyond us. It is a mystery that we cannot hem in with theological words. Nor should we try to.

Rather, we should ask ourselves, Are we awake to God's presence here in the sanctuary with us? At the table during family devotions? During the moments of our day when we are worried or thankful or tired? We cannot define God's presence, but we can sense it through the inner eye of our heart ("I pray also that the eyes of your heart may be enlightened," says Paul in Eph. 1:18). Are we awake to the awareness that in him we live and move and have our being? How is that awareness reflected in our worship?

Years ago while visiting in Solvang, California, our family went to a small Presbyterian church in the community. We were just entering the front doors when we heard the whirring, choppy sounds of a helicopter approaching. Looking up, we saw several helicopters circle above the church and land in a nearby field.

As we watched, ten or fifteen men got out—followed by the President and First Lady of the United States. They walked past us into the church, smiling and shaking hands. We followed in a daze.

Every eye was riveted to the pew in which the President sat. Every ear listened to the sermon with speculation as to what the President thought of it. We were keenly aware of his presence during the singing, during the responsive reading, during the time when everyone turned around to shake hands with neighbors.

I remember little of that worship service, but I will always carry with me this: the palpable awareness of the presence of the President of the United States.

How awake are we to God's presence? Perhaps less than we think. Sometimes the long habit of church attendance and the sameness of the liturgy lull us to sleep. Adults resign themselves to this quiet boredom; children, however, are more vocal about their dissatisfaction with a worship that excludes them.

Worship at First Church had begun. Bill sat with his wife and two children in the third pew from the front. He felt content. His catering business was going well, and by the following month he would be able to put an offer on the new building. On the way to church the family had driven by just to look at it.

The minister's salutation, the opening hymn, and the reading of the Law came and went. There was a liturgy of confession, which Bill didn't recite until his wife nudged him on the last line: "Lord, have mercy, Christ have mercy." It almost sounded Catholic to Bill.

The sermon was on Isaiah 6: "In the year that King Uzziah died, I saw the Lord seated on a throne, high and exalted, and the train of his robe filled the temple . . ."

Five-year-old Jobie had snuck his Transformers into church and was starting to fly them around and make guttural noises in his throat. Bill tapped him on the knee and shook his head, frowning. Jobie asked for a peppermint.

The sermon went longer than usual. Jobie kept kicking the Bible rack; occasionally he would sigh loudly and ask how much longer church was. Finally Bill gave him his watch. Jobie fiddled with the time and date until the sermon was over.

The elders came up to distribute bread and wine for the Lord's Supper. Bill had forgotten that today was communion Sunday; he had to call a client before noon to confirm some business, and with this added to the service he might not make it. The reading of the forms seemed interminable. As the congregation lifted the bread to their mouths, Bill noticed Jobie putting his hand to his mouth as well, with a peppermint. Bill shook his head at Jobie, frowning again.

Jobie sighed and got out his Transformer. He began to make battle noises, but they were drowned out by the closing hymn:

My God, how wonderful Thou art,
Thy majesty, how bright!
How beautiful Thy mercy seat
In depths of burning light.

Bill had a good voice and enjoyed singing. The organist played it well—not too slow, not too fast.

As the song ended, Jobie's Transformer was in the middle of a nosedive. Bill grabbed the Transformer and put it in his pocket.

"The Lord bless you and keep you . . ." Bill checked his watch. It said 5:30 a.m., Wednesday. He got Joan's attention and pointed to his wrist. She checked her watch and mouthed back to him, "Eleven-forty-five." Whew! Bill thought to himself. I can still reach that client before noon if we hurry home!

Bill herded his family into the car and beat the traffic jam out of the parking lot. On the way home, he looked in the rearview mirror at Jobie. "Young man, you had better learn to sit still in church. And don't fool around during communion."

"How come I can't have some bread too, Dad?"

"It's for grown-ups, that's all. You wait till you're in high school . . . then you'll understand."

Jobie threw his Transformer onto the floor of the back seat. "I hate church," he said.

How Might Fear Affect Our Worship?

This may seem like an odd question. We teach our children that God is love, that God accepts us through faith in Jesus. What does fear have to do with worship?

Perhaps in worship we fear the unknown and the unpredictable. This is especially true of North American Christians, who live in a well-planned, carefully structured society. We like to know where our paycheck comes from and how much we will make this month. We plan our vacations and our dentist appointments. We know what society expects of us, and we live within "normal" limits. If the car or washing machine breaks down, a mechanic can fix it. We know where we're supposed to be tomorrow, and at what time—it's written in our daily schedule book. Even our life expectancy has been plotted on medical graphs.

In the midst of this carefully constructed reality comes a God who is beyond our comprehension, a God who breaks in on our ordinary view of things and turns it upside down, a God who makes everything new. Jesus made this very clear. He puzzled the people of his day by saying that the rich are poor, and the poor are rich. "Happy are those who mourn," he said. "You cannot find your lives until you lose them," he told his followers. "Forget the wisdom of the wise, and become as children," he told the adults. God turns our ordered world topsy turvy.

As if that weren't bad enough, this unpredictable and unconventional God demands that we give everything we have and are as an act of worship. He's not satisfied with a percentage of our income after taxes and deductions; he wants *us*—bodies and all.

> Therefore I urge you, brothers, in view of God's mercy, to offer your bodies as living sacrifices, holy and pleasing to God— this is your spiritual act of worship. *Romans 12:1*

In worship we don't just tell God how nice he is and that it's been great knowing him. Worship goes far beyond that. We place ourselves completely at his command. He is Lord.

It is understandable that we shy away from this awareness. Like the young man who came to visit the Abba, we have learned how to say the right words comfortably, without the intensity of meaning that would put our lives on the line.

We fear that a change in lifestyle may be demanded of us. We fear having to give up our long-held habits, the comfortable ways that we've always done things. And, judging from Jesus' words in the gospels, we are probably quite right in suspecting this. Worship will bring us face to face with what it means to say, "Jesus is our

13

Lord." If it does not, we fall under the same condemnation as the Old Testament church:

> "These people come near to me with their mouth
>   and honor me with their lips,
>   but their hearts are far from me.
> Their worship of me
>   is made up only of rules taught by men."   *Isaiah 29:13*

We also fear that worship will change the way we see ourselves. Worship brings joy, but it also brings an awareness of our brokenness and ugliness in the presence of the God of holiness and beauty. When we come face to face with God, something changes. "Now my eyes have seen you," says Job. "Therefore I despise myself and repent in dust and ashes."

"Woe to me! I am ruined!" cries Isaiah. "For I am a man of unclean lips, and I live among a people of unclean lips, and my eyes have seen the King, the Lord Almighty."

The tax collector in the temple "stood at a distance. He would not even look up to heaven, but beat his breast and said, 'God, have mercy on me, a sinner.' "

Such an awareness of our sin and imperfection is unsettling, to say the least. Part of us fears and avoids it.

We also fear the people around us. If we show emotion, act in a spontaneous way, share something personal, or sing a little too heartily—what will they think? That we're getting a bit too spiritual or emotional? Will we offend them? Make them snicker? So we worship in such a way that no one can tell what the other is feeling and thinking. We stand up and sit down to sing hymns. We turn and smile and shake hands at the appropriate time. In doing all the right things, however, we remain insulated from the emotions, the questions, the pain, the joy of those worshiping around us. We become distanced from others—and also gradually distanced from the depth of our own experience with God.

Finally, we fear the spontaneity and directness that children bring to worship. Unknowingly, we slip the liturgy over our children like a straitjacket. We place our hands over their mouths and teach them to sit quietly, like good little adults. We praise them for silence and rebuke their noisily whispered comments. We frown on their laughter and hush their giggles. We fervently hope they don't embarrass us or annoy others. In the process, we teach them that worship is a thing to be endured, not a mystery and a joy to be experienced.

How Can Worship Activities Invite Us to Enter More Fully Into Worshiping God?

Behavioral scientists have discovered that the two major hemispheres of our brain—the right and the left—control very different functions of our behavior and learning. The left hemisphere handles speech, logic, analysis, math problems and grammar, abstract thinking, sorting things into categories, naming, and so on. It explains and reasons. It is constantly judging and evaluating reality.

The right hemisphere of the brain is more imaginative. It dominates the artistic part of us—the part that sings, dances, enjoys poetry and painting, creates crafts and stories. The right brain is the center of our intuition—that leap in logic we take "on a hunch." It's the part of our brain most active in our emotions, our dreams, our perception of beauty.

Normally, these two hemispheres work together in an extraordinarily complex way. We shift from right brain to left, and back again, depending on what the situation demands.

But our scientific, industrial culture favors the left brain—science, logic, reasoning. Our educational system heavily emphasizes left-brain thinking and skills. And so, all too often, has our theology.

In Reformed theology, we have highly developed skills for scholarly exegesis: analyzing Scripture, categorizing verses, writing doctrinal statements and creeds. This has been our major strength—left-brain activity. But we fall a little short on right-brain activities: mystery, stories, symbols, emotion, artistic creativity, and dreams.

Our worship reflects this preference for left-brain activity. The sermon (a speaking activity based on logic, analysis, and categorizing) is central. The bread and wine (the most powerful symbols in the service) are often brought out only once every three months. Except for the music (generally a right-brain activity), the service is talking (a left-brain activity): greeting, reading the law, reciting the creeds, responsive reading, sermon, congregational prayer, benediction. Some of this talking can contain symbol, metaphor, and story, of course. But by and large, left-brain activity dominates the service.

In depending so heavily on left-brain activities in worship, we suffer two losses. First, we lose part of ourselves. We may be interested, we may gain new ideas, we may grow in knowledge of the Scriptures—but we have lost the depth of insight and response that comes when our imaginations are set afire, our emotions stirred, our creativity touched, our five senses stimulated.

Second, we lose our children's involvement. Most children under the age of six or seven are unable to follow left-brain reasoning: logical argument, following the sequence of a train of thought, understanding abstract concepts. The lyrics to many of our hymns are beyond young children's vocabulary and level of understanding. Even children's sermons generally ask listeners to participate on an intellectual, cognitive level—not an affective, imaginative one. When such left-brain activity is the meat of the service, children are left out. The best they can hope to do is to sit quietly enough so as not to warrant punishment at the end of worship.

What would happen if we opened our worship to more right-brain activities? Can church and family worship take place through right-brain activity? How might we incorporate storytelling, ritual, visual symbols, colors and textures, body movement and dance, drama, role-playing, and the like?

We also need to ask who will benefit more from this balanced approach to worship—the children or the adults? We may be surprised at the answer!

How Is Worship Meant to Reflect the Kingdom of God?

We often think of "kingdom living" as getting our hands dirty in the world, struggling to bring peace and healing to our broken culture. We try to wrest at least part of our world out of Satan's stronghold. We try to establish God's kingdom however and wherever we can—in our work, in our relationships, in the darkness of our own hearts.

This is wearisome work at times. So God has given us a place to rest, a place where we can get as close to the reality of God's kingdom as anywhere else on this earth: the worship service. "Six days shall you labor," says God. On the seventh we are drawn to rest and worship.

The worship service and family worship have the potential to create an oasis from a world that is out of kilter. We can find rest in God's welcome and in the affirmation of his love. We can confess our failings and receive God's forgiveness. All can be healed and restored in worship.

More than that, we can recreate the kingdom in our worship service. We proclaim that God is the all-powerful King, even when the world around us refuses to recognize his authority and rule. We live in a way that seems odd to the world: confessing sin to each other, forgiving each other, honoring the weak, putting aside our own wills to listen to God's, singing in the face of sin and death. We create a whole new world in worship.

In worship, believers weekly recreate God's kingdom—a place where justice, mercy, kindness, and righteousness reign.

One question we need to ask is this: What is the place of children in the kingdom of God? And a second is this: Does our worship— family or church—reflect children's place in that kingdom?

"Let the little children come to me, and do not hinder them, for the kingdom of God belongs to such as these. I tell you the truth, anyone who will not receive the kingdom of God like a little child will never enter it." And he took the children in his arms, put his hands on them and blessed them.

Mark 10:14–16

SUGGESTIONS FOR GROUP SESSION

Opening

Be sure to read the introduction to this course (pages 5–8) with its emphasis on establishing an atmosphere in which people feel free to talk about their feelings, their memories, their ideas. Begin your first session together by taking time to introduce yourselves and tell a little about your families, especially if there are those in the group who may not know each other well. Also take turns answering this question: "Why am I interested in the subject of children and worship?"

Next, open with a brief prayer, asking God to guide your discussion and bring to mind the important questions the group needs to ask. It would be helpful to include in your prayer, if possible, some of the things you have shared in the exercise above (for example: helping our own children worship better, including children specifically in the worship service, enriching family worship).

For Discussion

1. Distribute pencils and paper. Allow three to five minutes to write down any words, phrases, or ideas that come to mind when you think of the word "worship." If you get stuck during this time and can't think of anything, keep writing the word "worship" on the page until something else comes to mind. Pens should not leave the page, and you should not stop writing until the time is up. After everyone is finished, choose one item on the list to share with the rest of the group. (If you wish to add a short explanation to your contribution, that's fine.)
2. Discuss the Abba story in the introduction to this course. This may be a difficult place for some to start, since it makes us take a hard look at ourselves. Be sensitive to possible reluctance to talk about this point. Was anyone moved by the story? At what places did the "aha" come, the moments of self-revelation or discovery? Where does the story connect with us personally? What does it have to do with worship?
3. Talk about Bill's experiences in church. If we identify at times with Bill's detachment and lack of awareness of the liturgy and how it

brings us into God's presence, should we feel guilty? Is it possible, even as adults, to pay attention, to "be awake" to God's presence, 100 percent of the time? Why or why not? What questions does Bill's story make us ask ourselves about the way we worship?

4. Discuss Jobie's church experience. What memories does this bring back of your own childhood experiences? Share some of your stories. What questions does Jobie's story make us ask ourselves about the way we worship?

5. Read and discuss your reactions to the following thoughts on worship from Robert Webber, author of *Worship Is a Verb:*

> I believe that worship communicates in two ways: verbally and symbolically . . . It is also important for us to remember that communication in words and symbols is two-way . . . This can be illustrated by a recent experience I had with my son who was home from college. We went out together for breakfast, and as fathers do, I began asking him questions about school—his teachers, classes, and social life. I didn't feel I was getting anywhere because he responded with short, terse answers. Conversation and communication were lacking, and I felt pained and frustrated. Finally I said, "John, you make me feel terrible. I've run out of questions. You're not conversing with me. There is no communication between us."
>
> John, who can talk when he wants to, realized what was happening, and he obviously cared about my feelings. So he leaned back and relaxed, and it wasn't long before we were communicating, not only in words and tone of voice, but with gestures and body language. Our communication around that table became open and real.
>
> In similar fashion I've often thought how it must pain and frustrate God when we remain passive and uninvolved in our worship when God wants to communicate with us through words and symbols, and longs for response through words and symbols from us. (90-91)

6. Have you ever considered how different personalities prefer and respond to different types of worship experiences? Read the following descriptions; which of the four—Mary, Mark, Al, or Alice—do you tend to identify with? Have you ever become frustrated or felt misunderstood because your way of finding meaning in worship differs from that of someone else? Is it possible to plan worship services that allow all of us—including

children—to experience and worship God in the way he created us to?

Mary Mary is a practical woman—neat, methodical, a real detail person. As a deacon, she enjoys budget keeping as well as watching over things around church that need attending to—the frayed carpet, the repainting of the sanctuary, families who need assistance. In worship, Mary is also very aware of surrounding details—the changing banners and colors of the liturgical seasons always add to her deep enjoyment of worship.

Mark Mark, Mary's husband, lives in a different world. Metaphor, poetry, and symbols fascinate him. He has a lively imagination and an intuitive approach to worship. He especially appreciates sermons which include stories, because he enjoys making the connections and fitting the sermon truths together into the larger web of meaning that holds his life together. As a valued member of the worship committee, Mark has an instinct for weaving the elements of worship together into a harmonious whole.

Al Al feels most at home in situations that call for logical, rational thinking; he prefers to remain as objective as he can in all dimensions of his life. His faith is structured on the creeds, and he likes the logical orderliness of their framework. In worship, Al enjoys following the reasoning in the pastor's sermon, and he most clearly senses God's presence when the preacher says something profound, something deeply truthful.

Alice Unlike her husband, Al, who feels uncomfortable with any show of emotion in worship, Alice thrives on anything having to do with relationships—with God, with family, with friends. She expresses her feelings easily and appreciates the kind of worship service which provides opportunity for personal, emotional response as well as time for fellowship and sharing of one's faith in God with other members.

Closing

End your session with a short time of silence during which group members can reflect on their own need to know and worship God. Conclude with a short prayer for those whose task it is to plan and lead services that include all of God's children, enabling each one to enter into meaningful worship.

SESSION TWO

A CHILD'S VIEW

Dear God,
I love you. I just want to let you know ahead of time that I'd like to be there with you in heaven.
Love always,
Sarah
(age 8)

Dear God,
I just learned how to spell R E L I G I O N.
I feel good. Now I am learning something else that we are. It is called P R E S S B U T A R R I U N.
Emily
(age 6)

Jesus,
I feel very near to you.
I feel like you are beside me all the time.
Please be with me on Thursday. I am running in a 3 mile race then. I will need all the speed in the world. If you are not busy with other things, maybe you could be at the starting line, the finish line, and everywhere in between.
Frankie
(age 11)

—*excerpts from David Heller's* Dear God *(Doubleday, 1987)*

Our family visited a rather traditional community church last Sunday to worship. I've been attending worship services like this one since I was four weeks old, so nothing was new—until I put on other glasses. I filtered out the adults and looked just at the kids. After the service, I wrote down what I had observed regarding the children's involvement in worship.

This is what I saw.

No member under twenty had an active part in leading the service. Throughout worship, the children were expected to sit quietly. There was an adult choir that sang during offertory and during communion. Adults distributed the communion elements and participated in the Lord's Supper; adults collected the offering.

Except for the music and communion (in which the children did not participate), the entire service consisted of speaking. The minister spoke and the people listened. The words he used were on a ninth- or tenth-grade reading level. He used one brief story as a sermon illustration to introduce the topic of Christ's atonement. Many words in the sermon were weighty, theological, and above the children's comprehension. The same was true for the hymns.

The children amused themselves as best they could—from the middle schooler who sat with glazed eyes, enduring the eternity of the sermon, to the kindergartner who twisted her mother's handkerchief into various shapes and used it to wave at her friends.

I thought about why the service had been the way it was. Guessing that the service had been planned and led by adults, I concluded that the adults had made certain assumptions about children and worship:

- Children are too young to worship God.
- God doesn't address children.
- Children have nothing to offer in worship.
- It's good discipline for children to learn to sit quietly through the service.
- Children interfere with the adults' worship.

In this course for adults on children and worship, we need to take a look at how many of these assumptions are ours as well. We don't often verbalize these assumptions, of course. But perhaps we don't have to. The role we assign to children in our public—and sometimes our family—worship speaks loudly enough. To some extent, it's likely that one or more of these assumptions are present in the kind of worship we bring our children to.

Are these assumptions about children true? What potential do children really have for participating in worship?

If we are serious about answering these questions, we need to take a closer look at who children are and how they learn, how they experience life.

Children Are Not Miniature Adults

Parents sometimes catch themselves saying sharply to their children, "Act your age!" As a general rule, the kids probably are. We adults just aren't sure what their age should be acting like.

We sometimes forget that children are not miniature adults (or even immature adults). In some ways, children are a different breed altogether. Eric Erikson and Jean Piaget, two widely recognized authorities on child development in Western society, have observed that children move through different stages of growth in their personalities and in their ways of learning. A summary of Erikson's and Piaget's discoveries will help us understand one of the greatest mysteries in God's creation: the child.

According to Erikson, each stage of childhood brings with it a major issue the child must deal with. These issues are social; they have to do with how children fit into the world around them. We're probably most familiar with the central issue of the adolescent's stage: finding his or her own unique identity. Young children, however, face social issues that are just as crucial.

In infancy, for example, the basic lesson children learn is trust. Do their parents (or grandparents or other caretakers) really care for them? Will their stomachs be filled when they cry with hunger? Will they be kept warm, protected from what frightens them, and find love instead of rejection? How much can they trust the world around them to nurture and care for them?

The issue of trust is foundational to the way each human being will approach life—even into his or her older years. Failure to bond with and trust an adult caretaker in the first year of life often produces antisocial behavior and severe emotional disorders in adults. Learning to trust is critical—especially to a developing relationship with God.

In early childhood (roughly ages one to three), children need to learn a sense of autonomy—that they are separate individuals from their parents and that they can choose to do some things and not others. Children must learn that they can exercise some control (in toilet training, for example) and can affect the world around them. If they are not able to do this, a sense of shame and doubt dogs their developing personalities. They begin to doubt their self-worth and the worth of the world around them.

From ages three to six, children develop a sense of initiative. If they're allowed to use their newly acquired skills of using a scissors or riding a tricycle, for example, they will glow with the excitement of having done something on their own. If they're allowed to express their thoughts and ideas through action, they learn that they can take initiative and that their ideas are worth expressing.

Stifling their expression of ideas through action or play, however, creates a sense of guilt in children, a sense that they are not acceptable. Children who are criticized for their efforts, especially at this stage, will have a hard time taking initiative as adults. The feeling of being "not right" or unacceptable is one that many adults struggle with; and it often begins at this crucial stage of life.

Children of elementary school age (ages six to twelve) work to acquire a sense of industry. During this period of intense learning, children like to try many different activities and pursue a myriad of interests. Though the activities and interests may be short-lived, this stage of industrious activity develops children's sense of adequacy and self-worth.

Keeping kids from pursuing these interests or criticizing them when they try out new activities pushes them toward feelings of inferiority. Perhaps these years are the *most* crucial for children to not only learn about worship but also take an active part in it.

Knowing how children develop socially is one step in understanding how children fit into worship. But we also need to know how children think. Here Piaget's research is helpful.

Piaget asserts that in the first year of life, the child is busy discovering that there are other objects in the world, things and people separate from himself or herself. An infant can sense, for example, that being in church is different from being at home. In this early stage of awareness the infant also senses whether church is a warm, safe, loving place or one that is threatening and unpleasant. These early impressions can linger through the later childhood years.

In the second and third years, the child begins to recognize objects and identify them by name. But children this age can't classify these objects into groups very well; they are just beginning to realize, for example, that two separate animals can be of the same species. They recognize church furnishings by touch and sight—pews, pulpit, stained glass, communion table, banners. They are aware of worship that is rich in color, movement, song, and objects.

At ages three through six, children are somewhat more able to see relationships between objects they're familiar with. For example, they recognize hymn singing, prayer, the sermon, and the baptismal ceremony as all parts of the service. But why one follows another or how these are all linked together is beyond children of this age. They aren't able to follow logical reasoning to any great degree. They also don't understand much of the adult language they hear. "Low in the Gravy Lay" and "Gladly, the Cross-Eyed Bear" are two examples of the mistakes children are prone to make at this age.

However, children at this age also have a delightful imagination, one unencumbered by logic. They can take an image or symbol and with their imagination fly with it in any direction. Stories are extremely important, though the children will probably remember single episodes or images from the story rather than the entire sequence of events.

Another interesting part of this stage: three-, four-, and five-year-olds generally don't have a clear sense of moral conscience; they're likely to say they shouldn't do something "because Mom or Dad says so," not "because it's wrong."

Children this age also have a short attention span and need to move around; they are developing their motor skills and find it almost impossible to sit still for an hour—or even twenty minutes. But they're able to memorize sentences and can take part in worship by reciting certain responses and prayers or singing certain hymns, especially the refrains.

School-age children (ages six to twelve) have a much greater ability to see relationships between objects, to see the "whole picture," to think in historical sequence. They want to know why certain things happen in the worship service. Greater vocabulary, better reading skills, and a longer attention span enable these children to understand and take part in the service. They can use the hymnbook and the Bible, though much of the language and meaning may be beyond them. Again, their thinking is more stimulated by story and by images than by logical, rational discourse— though this is also true of adolescents and most adults.

This abbreviated description of how children develop socially and mentally should help us understand that young children are not simply smaller, less mature copies of the adults that they worship with. In some ways, children live in a different world from adults. For most of us, it's been too many years since we've inhabited that world. We need to be reminded again not only of children's limitations but also of their immense capabilities.

With this background material in mind, then, let's examine those assumptions mentioned at the beginning of this session.

Are Young Children Ready to Worship God?

Yes, young children *are* ready to worship God—if they're given an opportunity. They have a marvelous capacity for wonder, for drawing close to the numinous—a sense of the holy, of the presence of God. Too often, however, we simply try to keep them busy with lots of activity, movement, and crafts—or we require them to sit still and be quiet without including them in what's going on. Given the chance to respond to God in a quiet, focused way, however, children reveal a deep joy and a marvelous capacity for sensing God's love and presence.

Our inner-city church tried a new approach to children and worship several years ago, inviting the neighborhood children to join in. The first few sessions there were no Bible stories or crafts; the children were simply taught how they must walk and talk in the worship center (quietly and with respect), how they must "get ready to meet God," what the lighted candle signified (the presence of Christ), how the Bible was to be treated (with respect as the Word of God), and so on.

These usually rowdy kids sat enthralled in these first sessions. Something deep inside, some inner yearning for God and for the quiet order in which to worship him, was touched in them. They left the building with great excitement, and we overheard them telling their friends on the street, "You've got to come with us next week! This is really great stuff!"

The children multiplied, till we had 30–40 children packed into one room. The rituals, which had been carefully explained at the beginning, were followed each week. Children who had forgotten the rules of behavior or who found it difficult to sit still were placed beside adult helpers during the story. A sense of expectancy grew as the storyteller began. After the story, each child was invited to draw or color or make some kind of art response to the story. The room was quiet; the children were absorbed in their quiet, uninterrupted response to God.

I use this example from our church because it surprised me to see how willing the children were to participate quietly, with focused attention, when they knew that they were in the presence of something really important, something that spoke to them of God.

Children have a simplicity and directness in prayer that reveals a surprising intimacy with God. Sofia Cavalletti, who pioneered a new approach to children and worship, recorded the following sentence prayers of thanksgiving offered by a group of three- to six-year-olds:

Jesus, you are my shepherd.
You are my savior.
Jesus, you are my father.
You are my friend.
Jesus, you are the king of the world.
Jesus, you help me, thank you.
Jesus, I thank you for giving us all these things.

Jesus, I thank you for making us live and letting us play with
our friends.
Thank you, Jesus, for creating us.

Even those children who have never been taught about God
seem to have an intuitive awareness of his existence. Cavalletti tells
of a three-year-old girl who had grown up in an atheistic home,
without a trace of religious influence:

> The child did not go to nursery school; no one at home, not
> even her grandmother, who was herself an atheist, had ever
> spoken of God; the child had never gone to church. One day
> she questioned her father about the origin of the world:
> "Where does the world come from?" Her father replied, in a
> manner consistent with his ideas, with a discourse that was
> materialistic in nature; then he added, "However, there are
> those who say that all this comes from a very powerful being,
> and they call him God." At this point the little girl began to run
> like a whirlwind around the room in a burst of joy, and ex-
> claimed: "I knew what you told me wasn't true; it is Him, it is
> Him!"

God has given even the least of these, his children, the capacity
to know and love him. "For since the creation of the world God's
invisible qualities—his eternal power and divine nature—have been
clearly seen, being understood from what has been made . . . "
Rom. 1:20

Do we believe this? Then we must rethink the ways in which we
ask our children to participate in worship services. Our children's
capacity for worship should be nurtured, not stifled, when we gather
as God's people to renew and refresh our relationship with him and
with each other.

Does God Speak to Children?

We need only to read the gospels to discover that children are
very important to Christ (Matt. 18:1–5; 19:13–15; Mark 9:33–37;
10:13–16; Luke 9:46–48; 18:15–17). Children occupy a central place
in his kingdom and in his heart. In fact, when the adults are
misbehaving, Jesus puts forward a small child as the role model.

Certainly, then, God speaks to these children. Would he not take
great delight in meeting them also in worship, putting his hands on
them also and blessing them? We must admit that we adults have
been rather inconsistent. The worship services we plan and lead
always include the Word of God—but it is largely spoken by adults
to adults. Most of it goes over the children's heads. Even children's
sermons are often inappropriate to the child's ability to reason,

making connections that children can't understand. Some are simply moralistic stories that tell children how to behave.

Using the insights into childhood development presented above, what can we discover about the ways in which God might speak to children?

First, God speaks to children through a medium they can understand and respond to. As noted earlier, that medium includes story, symbol, imagery, song, color, movement, and ritual. A twenty-minute sermon may be fine for adults—and a vital, central part of their worship. But it does not address children, even elementary-age children, in the primary ways that God has created them to learn about and respond to him.

Children learn best when learning becomes something they can touch, taste, see, feel, and hear. The language of the Judeo-Christian heritage is rich in signs, symbols, and images that can help children express the many dimensions of their relationship to God. These signs invite young and old alike into the mystery of the experience of God. And children, even when they may not be able to verbalize meaning, find these images deeply satisfying, an inner language that helps them experience the mystery of God.

Yes, God undoubtedly addresses our children. The question is, do our worship services—and our family worship—allow God to address children in a way that they can understand?

Must Children Be Seen and Not Heard?

"It's good discipline for children to learn to sit quietly through the service." That's probably true. It's also good discipline to finish the food on one's plate, to clean one's room, to brush one's teeth after every meal.

But is "good discipline" what worship is all about?

It is true that children need to learn the social graces, to learn respect for others and proper behavior in a group of people. But worshiping God should not be the same kind of disciplinary experience as eating all their peas or picking up their socks. It's not meant to be an unpleasant experience that they do simply because it's good for them.

Yet that's what we may unwittingly be teaching our children in the kind of service described at the beginning of this chapter.

Children, you see, learn a little from the words that we speak to them. But they learn much more from our actions and our attitudes. Sometimes the fiercely whispered "Sit still and be quiet!" is well-deserved. But is that the prevailing attitude toward children expressed in our corporate and family worship?

Here's where the issue of process versus content comes in. We can teach a child *content* through words: "You are loved," we tell him. But if the *process* of our teaching communicates something else—we never touch the child, never praise him for what he does, never listen to his ideas, never speak warmly to him and tousle his hair—we have given him an even deeper, clearer message of unacceptance and isolation.

We can teach our children through *words* that Jesus loves them, that God values them highly, that they are precious to him. But when all we ask of them in worship is to sit still and not bother the adults, what do they learn through the *process* of our worship? When we don't give them opportunity to express their faith and worship in words and songs that they can understand, what are we really teaching them?

We sometimes forget how deeply children are affected by relationships. Adults can leave a worship service feeling spiritually fed by the proclaimed Word, even when they haven't said more than a brief "good morning" to anyone around them. But for children, relationships with each other and with adults are what make up the experience of church. That's why the *process* of our worship service speaks so much louder than the *content*, as far as children are concerned.

Our neglect of children in the service may have a long-term effect on their feelings of worth in God's eyes and acceptance within the fellowship of the church. Look again, for example, at Erikson's insights into the critical social issues of a child's development. Do we encourage autonomy in our two- to three-year-olds? Do we allow them to have some effect, however small, on the worship environment?

Are our three- through six-year-olds given a chance to take the initiative in the worship service, to work with their lively imaginations and express what they've experienced in worship? Or does our hand over their mouth communicate a feeling that they're not all right, that their questions and responses and needs in worship are unacceptable?

Do we allow our elementary-age children to apply their varied interests and their need for industry to the experience of worship? Or do we give them the feeling that they're too young, that they'll probably make too many mistakes, and that their contributions won't add much to the adults' sense of worship anyway?

Content versus process. Basically, it comes down to the old adage "Actions speak louder than words." When we cling to the idea that it's good discipline for children to sit quietly through a service geared to adults, we're teaching our children that worship is an unpleasant duty—one in which they don't have much to offer.

What Do Children Have to Offer?

Worship and the kingdom of God are inextricably intertwined. The first session of this course concluded with the thought that in worship we are able to create a part of God's kingdom anew each week.

Children are important in worship in part because they are able to teach adults how to receive that kingdom. "I tell you the truth, anyone who will not receive the kingdom of God like a little child will never enter it." The capacity for wonder, the ability to perceive the numinous presence of God, a lively imagination, the ability to enter into religious symbols and imagery, an unquestioning trust in a loving and all-powerful God—these are things we adults may have lost and forgotten. We need our role models in the kingdom.

Later sessions will deal with suggestions on how to allow children to participate more fully in worship. But before we look at those suggestions, we need to deal with the fear that children will disrupt our worship if we loosen the straitjacket of the liturgy we've slipped over them. Are we afraid? Perhaps we're uncomfortable with children's unpredictability, with their enthusiasm and spontaneity. What will these do if unleashed in a worship service?

We may also fear having to give up our adult ways of worship. For one thing, we've grown comfortable with them. But we also don't want to replace the meaty, more challenging presentation of God's Word with watered-down, simplistic sermonettes for children. We have come to love and appreciate the great hymns of the Christian faith. Does including the children in worship mean giving up all of this?

Fears about change are legitimate. Change always means at least a little pain or discomfort. However, change doesn't necessarily mean taking out elements of the service that we find helpful as adults. It may mean simply adding other elements.

We can add to our worship things that children can respond to— the richness of imagery, ritual, color, movement, story, and symbol. The bonus is that adults can also respond to these things. In fact, these are the very elements that help balance the left-brain, cerebral worship activities that have dominated our services in the past.

Adults have an often untapped capacity for imagination and wonder, a need for touch and for relationship, a readiness to respond to symbol and ritual. Adults' ears also perk up at stories, allegories, word pictures, and metaphors that make the "meat" of the sermon come alive.

We can also add activities that invite *everyone* to participate, to bring a special gift or insight to worship. A time of sharing, a common prayer time in which all participate, the opportunity to suggest songs—these are all concrete ways to teach children about the priesthood of all believers in worship. It will teach the same thing to the adults.

For these reasons a conscious effort to include children will enrich, not detract from, adult worship. The words "Children should be seen and not heard" did not come from our Lord's mouth. "Let the little children come to me," he told his group of reluctant adults. He knew that the children could teach them something they might have forgotten: how to enter the kingdom of God.

SUGGESTIONS FOR GROUP SESSION

Opening

For openers, try this activity: Arrange your chairs so that there are some empty spaces between them. Ask a few members of the group to sit on the floor in those empty spaces. Hand out songbooks to the people sitting on chairs, but give none to those on the floor. Group members sitting on chairs should keep those on the floor quiet and still. People seated on chairs may talk quietly among themselves; those on the floor should be discouraged from making any noise. If they get restless and can't see the discussion leader, tell them to be patient—the session will be over in an hour or so.

You may want to choose an unfamiliar song from the songbook so that those sitting on the floor won't be able to sing along.

It should sink in, of course, that you are asking some adults to experience something of what children experience in an average Sunday worship service. After you feel the experience has gone on long enough, let the "children" get up and sit with the rest of the adults. Take time to talk about your reactions to this experience.

Continue by singing a song that emphasizes our identity as God's children and our trust in his care, such as "Children of the Heavenly Father." As you offer a prayer for your time together, ask God's Spirit to remind you during this time of the ways in which all believers are as children before God.

For Discussion

1. Read aloud Jesus' words from Mark 9:33–37 and Mark 10:13–16. Imagine yourself as a child present in one of these encounters with Christ. How would you feel being there? What would you learn about yourself from Jesus? How would you learn it? What would you learn about Jesus? How would you learn it?
2. Think of instances from your childhood, adolescence, or even your adult years in which you learned much more from some-

one's actions than from their words. Which teachers had the greatest impact on you? Why? Was it due to the content of the lesson or the way in which they taught it?

Now think about your church services. What might children be learning about themselves from the process of worship at your church? What do you want them to learn?

3. Read the following illustration aloud:

A bishop came to watch a religious instruction class of four-to six-year-olds in his church. The children did their activity as usual, working with figures from the parable of the good shepherd. He noticed the children taking the sheep from the sheepfold and placing these around a kind of altar, on which the good shepherd had been placed, next to the communion chalice and plate.

He listened to their comments as they did this quiet activity: that they are the sheep, that the good shepherd takes us places where "we are happy," that the good shepherd meets us especially at communion, that "he comes just to be with us." One child said, "Let's put away the good shepherd statue; there's the bread and wine. It is the same."

As the children gathered round, one of the teachers said, "The Father gave us Jesus. What can we give him?" Earlier the children had made and cut out two paper hands with the palms face-up. Some of them got up now and brought the hands, and they began to place on those hands things that represented their offering—the figure of the good shepherd, a wooden figure of a person to show their own personal involvement, the figure of a sheep from the good shepherd parable.

Everyone brought something, except for the bishop. Finally one child turned to him and asked, "And your sheep?" The bishop, visibly moved, took a sheep and put it in the palms of the paper hands. Later he commented on what impressed him most: the children's ability to speak about such profound things in so natural and serious a way.
—condensed from *The Religious Potential of the Child*, 88–89.

Share with the group an experience you have had with a child or children which moved you to marvel, as the bishop did, at children's ability to respond to God in a profound way.

4. Divide into groups of three or four. Together with your group, draw up a list of qualities Jesus may have had in mind when he said, "Unless you change and become as little children, you can never enter the kingdom of heaven." Pick out three or four qualities that you can all agree on and share them with the larger group.

Then answer this question as a group: How can we encourage children to share in worship in ways that help us observe these qualities?

Closing

Read John 10:1–18 aloud (with one person reading the entire passage or members taking turns with the verses). Pause for five minutes of quiet time to reflect on the imagery and the symbols presented in these verses.

Then write down on a piece of paper the ways in which the images connect with your own faith experience. For example, imagine the wolf. What does it look like? What does the hired hand look like? The shepherd? What in your life reminds you of the wolf? When have you ever heard the voice of the shepherd? What feelings or emotions do you have as you read these verses? Why?

Discuss your reactions to the parable with the group. What part of your brain was engaged more—left or right? Was it enjoyable? How would it compare to listening to a lecturer spell out five ways in which Jesus is like a shepherd to his church? Do both activities have a place in worship? How would children respond to working with this imagery?

SESSION THREE

A HISTORICAL PERSPECTIVE

Children are the question-askers of our families—especially when it comes to God and to the stories they hear from the Bible. Children are surprised, amused, awed, and sometimes a little skeptical of what they learn in the Old and New Testaments. With the wealth of wonderful stories—about floods, giants, battles, the sun standing still, three men in a fiery furnace, shipwrecks and escapes from prison—they are always full of questions.

From earliest biblical history, the role of asking questions seems to have fallen to the children. For centuries after the escape from Egypt, on Passover night the youngest child of the family has asked the all-important question "Why is this night different from any other?" When white flakes of sweet bread fell for the first time in the desert, children awoke their parents that morning with hands full of it and gave it its name: *manna*, meaning "What is it?" When their fathers and older brothers laid the twelve stones of the altar across the Jordan, the children were ready with their questions: "Why are you doing that? What do those stones mean? Why are there twelve?"

Children raced up and down the big blocks that slowly went up to form the walls of the new temple under Solomon's reign. "What is this part going to be?" They played along the rivers of Babylon, listening to the slow, sad songs of the exile that their parents were singing. "Why are you crying, Abba?" the children said. "Why don't we sing happy songs?"

The children who lived near the Jordan River stared at John the Baptist's outlandish clothes and demanded to know why he was making people get wet in the river. "What does 'repent' mean, Abba? What is the kingdom of God?"

When they came on the Sabbath to the synagogue to worship with their families, they saw a man named Jesus touch the old man's withered arm and heal it. "How did he do that, Abba?" they asked. "Is he God?"

Throughout the Bible, children are everywhere—restless, questioning, awe-struck, pestering, curious. From Israel's earliest worship as families and tribes, to the early Christian church's secret gatherings in house churches and underground caves, the children were present—a vital part of the worshiping community. Because the children were always questioning and always learning, they helped the adults explain their faith and redefine its meaning for their particular time.

This session looks at the way children were taught to know and worship God, both in the Old and New Testaments. It highlights the child's role of question-asker and focuses on two ways children learned true worship of God: through being included in the worshiping community and by being confronted with a religion rich in imagery, symbolism, and ritual.

Learning by Inclusion

Imagine that you have been born to Jewish parents during the times of the Old Testament kings. This may be a bit difficult, since you are a twentieth-century product, brought up by good European or African or Korean or whatever stock. But give it a try. Think small (put yourself between the ages of three and six) and imagine olive skin and dark hair and eyes.

Your mother has just called you in to prepare for the Sabbath meal. "Hurry!" she says. "The sun is almost down!" As you wash your feet inside the doorway, you watch your mother lighting the Sabbath lamp, a sign that evening is falling and the Sabbath day of rest has begun.

You carefully follow the ritual washing before meals, remembering what your father said when you asked, "Why do we wash this special way before we eat, Abba?" His reply: "We cannot pray to the one God with hands that are stained with dirt or with disobedience. Only clean hands, hands that are full of good deeds, can be lifted in praise to the One."

The meal is the best of the week, kept warm in the oven so that your mother and sister will have no work on the Sabbath. But before you begin eating, your father chants softly, singing the psalms of praise he learned from others as he went to Jerusalem each year for the great feasts. As you remember words and phrases, you join in, almost forgetting the steaming food on the table before you.

Father takes the two small loaves of freshly baked bread and breaks them. Passing the pieces around the table, he bids all of you to eat as a sign of your thanks to God. Pouring wine into a cup, he thanks the Holy One for the fruit of the vine and passes it around the table.

After your meal together, your father turns to your mother and speaks of his love for her. Then he rises and places his hands on you and your brother and sister in turn, pronouncing a blessing from God. You love the feel of his hand and the gentleness of his voice.

Your own voice is cracked and a little unsteady as you in turn pronounce the Sabbath blessing you learned from your mother a few weeks ago. But your father smiles and nods approvingly. Now you can leave the table.

Your brother and you have learned not to argue on the Sabbath, so you sit in the doorway, speaking in quiet voices about the prospect of going to Jerusalem. The grape harvest will be finished this week. That means it's almost time for the Feast of Ingathering, or the Festival of Booths. Along with every other male in Israel, you are required to be present at the Temple for the feast.

"Why do we have to live in booths?" you ask.

Your father's response is gentle. "Has not Moses written the words of the Lord to us in this matter?" Your father recites from the Torah by heart:

> So beginning with the fifteenth day of the seventh month, after you have gathered the crops of the land, celebrate the festival to the Lord for seven days . . . Live in booths for seven days: All native-born Israelites are to live in booths so your descendants will know that I had the Israelites live in booths when I brought them out of Egypt. I am the Lord your God.

"And you, my youngest son, will help me make the best booth our family has yet lived in during the week of Succoth. Each branch will represent one of the wonderful things the Lord God has done in your own life and in the history of your people.

"Come, I have stories to tell you, stories that you will remember and tell to your own children."

Inclusion in Family Worship

In the warmth and security of the family, the Jews taught their children about the worship of God. The Shema, that passage from Deuteronomy that became the heart of Old Testament religion and life, mentions the child as an integral part of the faith community. Each Israelite family repeated the Shema as part of its daily worship.

Hear, O Israel: The Lord our God, the Lord is one. Love the Lord your God with all your heart and with all your soul and with all your strength. These commandments that I give you today are to be upon your hearts. Impress them on your children. Talk about them when you sit at home and when you walk along the road, when you lie down and when you get up. Tie them as symbols on your hands and bind them on your foreheads. Write them on the door frames of your houses and on your gates.

In the Israelite household, worship and education were intertwined. In fact, education in Israel was primarily religious. Parents taught their children how to run a household, of course, along with the family trade. But woven into the fabric of this education was the central proclamation: "Hear, O Israel: The Lord our God, the Lord is one." Everyday matters like food preparation, diet, clothing, lending money, harvesting crops, and medical care were governed by special rules that reminded the people that they belonged to God.

The parents' teaching was often prompted by their children's questions. Throughout the Old Testament books of the law there runs the repeated phrase "And when your children ask you . . . " Many of the religious rites God commanded his people to observe were designed not only to remind the adults of their commitment to God but also to draw out the questions of their children.

In this way each generation was taught the ways of God and the faith was kept alive, fresh, and meaningful. Without God's command to teach children the meaning behind the actions and symbols, the Jewish faith would have degenerated into superstition and empty ritual.

Certainly the Israelites were no shining example of obedience and devotion to God. They often failed to follow God's way of passing faith on from one generation to the next. But, as God had intended, enough of their religion and worship was woven into family life so that the Jews never lost their religious identity in the face of centuries of oppression and devastation that would have wiped out almost any other culture.

Inclusion in Religious Rites

Since the home was the center of worship and education, parents were the primary teachers. They taught in part by *including* their children in all religious activities—Sabbath preparation and obser- vance, synagogue worship, feast days, religious holy days.

Children were required to attend synagogue services on the Sabbath after they were four years old. Boys under twelve years of age could read from the Torah at the synagogue. Here the entire family took part in prayers and singing psalms. They listened to the wise men of the community expound on the truths of the Torah, the books of the law.

But even before the custom of worshiping at the synagogue began, Jewish life was filled with feasts and religious holidays that were exciting events for children. For example, though only males were required to go up to Jerusalem for the three religious fes- tivals—Passover, the Feast of Booths, and Pentecost—wives and children often joined fathers and uncles in the trek to Jerusalem. In New Testament times, some two and one half million people con- verged on Jerusalem during these feast days.

Children were an integral part of these three main religious festivals. The Passover celebration was centered on the family meal together. The youngest child played an important role in this special meal, asking the leading question: "Why is this night different from all others?" Each year the father explained carefully to his family the meaning of the Passover and the history of God's deliverance in Egypt. The children also assisted their parents in the week before Passover, searching the house for any bit of leavened bread that might have fallen into cracks or corners. The night of the Passover meal the children and parents dressed in their best clothes, as if ready to depart on a journey. The whole family recited the events of their ancestors' flight from Egypt.

During the Feast of Booths, or Tabernacles (also called Succoth), the family gathered boughs and made booth-like tents. Adults and children alike lived in these booths the entire week of the festival, remembering the Israelites' long wandering in the desert.

The feast of Pentecost, which took place in the spring at the end of the barley harvest and in the middle of the wheat harvest, also involved the entire family. Children helped their parents reap a small field of grain, separate the wheat from the chaff, and grind the grain. The mother and daughters used the flour to bake two huge loaves, which were then waved to the sky in thanksgiving to the God who made their land fertile and their crops plentiful. This festival was linked with the remembrance of God's giving of the Law on Mount Sinai, and the children listened with their parents as the Law was read and celebrated.

Children were also present when their parents brought animals to be sacrificed. The children heard their parents' murmured confession of guilt. They watched as the priest laid his hand on the animal's head, slit its throat, and collected the blood in a bowl. Later, at home, the flood of questions came: "What did you do wrong, Abba?" "Why did you have to take the best goat of our flock?" "Why do we have to have blood in order for God to forgive us?"

Because of their presence at the sacrifices, feasts, and religious celebrations of their day, children asked questions that made their elders think. Their questions demanded careful thought and helped reshape their parents' theology to fit the time in which they lived and worshiped. In this way, the child became as vital to worship and religious education as the adult. Both needed each other to make sense of their common history and of the nature of the God they served and worshiped.

Inclusion from Birth

It's important to note that children were included in the Jewish covenant community from birth. Children did not have to profess a certain standard of faith or set of beliefs before being declared Israelites. They were included because they had been born into a Jewish family—and into the larger Israelite family, the people of God. Their inclusion was not based on anything they had done or said. It was a gift, given by God to all the descendants of Abraham.

The early Christian church also included young children in its fellowship. Family worship was the norm. From what we can gather from the scant records of the first-century church, it seems probable that children of believing parents were baptized along with them. Certainly by the second century, infant baptism had become the accepted practice. As with the rite of circumcision in the Old Testament, baptism was taken as a sign of the child's inclusion in the covenant community.

According to many reports, children were also included at the Lord's table from birth. Through the thirteenth century, children and infants were given the bread and the wine immediately upon being baptized and after the bishop laid his hands on them in the rite of confirmation.

After the thirteenth century, the Western church began to give communion to older children only, gradually raising the age of those partaking to eleven or twelve. This came about because the rites of baptism and confirmation were gradually being separated. Local priests were able to baptize the children of their villages, but only the bishop was authorized to confirm them. As the church spread, bishops found it difficult to be on hand for all the baptisms in their areas. In some villages the bishop did not come to visit more than once every two or three years. So, as a matter of convenience, the children were confirmed at an older age when the bishop was present. Thus the practice of infant communion gradually died out in the Western church. (The Eastern Orthodox Church still retains the practice of infant baptism, confirmation, and communion.)

Also, as the doctrine of the Eucharist began to crystallize, most churches taught that the wine and bread were indeed Christ's body and blood in the most literal sense. This led to a very real fear: What if the body and blood of Christ were profaned by being spilled or dropped onto the ground? Because of this fear, some priests took communion on behalf of their entire congregation, not wanting some person to accidentally spill the sacred elements. Children were considered especially prone to this kind of accident and were often excluded from the table. Again, however, this was not the practice of the early church.

In both Old and New Testaments, the worshiping church included its children in family and public worship. In circumcision and the Passover meal, in baptism and the Lord's Supper, children were invited and welcomed as joint heirs with all of God's covenant children. This is one way that children grew in the knowledge and worship of God.

Learning Through Imagery, Symbolism, and Ritual

Another way in which children learned to know and worship God was through the richness of the religious ritual, the actions and symbols and memorials that reminded the Old and New Testament believers of who God was.

God's laws had been preserved for Israel in oral and later in written tradition, of course. But God knew that people learned best when the spoken word was accompanied by visual signs, by actions, by visible reminders. From the animals whose throats were slit on the altar to the bread and wine we serve at Communion— God gives his people visual reminders that speak of who He is and remind us of our relationship to him.

Old Testament worship was full of this imagery—so much so, in fact, that a detailed discussion would fill a book. Let's take a random look at some of the rituals and symbols that enriched the worship of adults and children alike.

Sabbath Observance

The most frequent and regular religious activity in Jewish life (outside of daily prayers) was the Sabbath observance. On the seventh day of the week, everything in Israel shut down. God had commanded that the Sabbath be a day of complete rest for the people of Israel. The Sabbath was extremely important in God's eyes.

And no wonder. For it stood as a reminder of God's two most spectacular acts in world history up till that time: the creation of the world and Israel's deliverance from Egypt.

When the children complained, "Why can't we do *anything* on the Sabbath?" the parents were to explain that the Sabbath is a reminder that God created the world in six days—and rested on the seventh (Ex. 31:17).

And when the children asked, "But can't the servants cook for us today?" the parents responded by recalling that God had led their ancestors out of slavery in Egypt and gave them rest (Deut. 5:15). Each Sabbath was a history lesson, an inescapable reminder of God's power and faithfulness as creator and deliverer. The Sabbath-rest also served as a symbol of the salvation-rest to come in Jesus (Heb. 4).

The Festival of Trumpets

In the autumn of every year (the first day of the month Tishri), silver trumpets sounded at dawn, thin and bright, over the walls of sleeping Jerusalem.

Throughout the day, ram's horn trumpets were blown. No one did any work; it was a day of rest and of sacrifices. The Festival of Trumpets had become a day of self-examination in Israel, a time to ask how one's life measured up to God's law. Hearing the shrill trumpet blast, young children clutched at their parents' robes and asked, "What is that noise?"

If the parents were God-fearing Israelites, they would answer, "The trumpets are good, child. They are sounded at the beginning of each month and especially at the beginning of the civil year to do three things. First, they are blown so that God will hear their sound and remember his covenant with us, the descendants of Abraham. Second, they are blown loudly to frighten away Satan, the dark one who brings death and evil. And third, they wake up any Israelites who are sleepy with sin, calling them to awaken and obey God's law once more."

The Day of Atonement

The Day of Atonement was a climax to the religious year in Israel. It was a spiritual spring cleaning, a time when the high priest made atonement not only for Israel's sins but also for those of the entire priesthood. Thus cleansed, everyone could begin the year anew.

The day was full of ritual and sacrifice, including the slaughter of a young bull for the priests' sins, followed by a ceremony involving two goats. First, the high priest laid his hands on the neck of the bull and confessed his sins and those of his household in the hearing of all the people. Watching, the children saw that sin and death go hand in hand.

One goat, chosen for the sin offering of the people, was slaughtered in the sight of the people and its blood was collected in a bowl. The priest then dipped his fingers in the blood from the bull and the goat and sprinkled it onto the great altar seven times to cleanse it from all the uncleanness of Israel's sins during the past year. Blood makes things clean again, the children learned.

The goat that remained was called the scapegoat. When the high priest was finished sprinkling the blood of the first goat, he laid his hands over the head of the second goat and named the sins of Israel—wickedness, rebellion, idolatry, stubbornness, disobedience, profanity. That goat was then led away into the wilderness, bearing the sins of the entire nation. And the children learned that God had given a way to atone for sins, to clear consciences, to start anew.

Feast of Tabernacles and Simchat Torah

The week-long festival that fell at the end of the grape harvest was known as the feast of Tabernacles, or Booths. Each Jewish family was to gather branches from the hill country and construct three-sided tents, like those their ancestors lived in while traveling from Egypt to Canaan.

Even more delightful, however, is the ritual that grew up around the last day of the festival—an especially festive day. The rabbis used the following parable to teach the meaning of this day:

> God is like a king who invites all his children to a feast to last for just so many days; when the time comes for them to depart, he says to them: "My children, I have a request to make of you. Stay yet another day; your departure is difficult for me."

This day, Simchat Torah, was probably the most joyous day of the entire year. It was a mighty celebration of the written Scriptures. As men, women, and children sang and danced their way around the synagogue, little ones learned that the written Word brings great joy and happiness; it is to be treasured and loved.

The Passover

The Passover festival took ordinary things from everyday life and gave them special meaning. Leaven, used in daily baking, was forbidden during this time; it was associated with evil and hypocrisy. During the week of Passover, the family ate unleavened bread to remember the haste with which their ancestors had left Egypt.

The Passover meal included a lamb, sacrificed and then roasted, to remind the people of the sacrificial lamb by whose blood they had been spared from the angel of death in Egypt. The bitter herbs eaten with the meat were to help Israel remember the bitterness of slavery under the Egyptians. Later the Israelites added the custom of dipping vegetables in salt water to remember the tears of their ancestors. A cup of red wine symbolized the joy of God's deliverance from slavery.

Baptism

In the early church, baptism took the place of circumcision as a sign of membership in the community of God's people. Baptism was not performed indoors, with only believers looking on, as it is in churches today. Rather, it was a public declaration of one's faith in Jesus, done out in the open. As far as we can tell from Scripture, it was not uncommon for entire households to be baptized at one time—adults and children alike.

The water of baptism served as a powerful symbol, partly because water was such a familiar and necessary part of life. One image connected to baptism was that of washing—washing clean from dirt, from sin, from guilt. Children, who had scrubbed their own dirty hands often enough and had watched their mothers wash their robes in the rivers and streams, knew that water made things clean.

Immersion in the waters of baptism also carried another image, however: the image of death and burial. Going under the water, believers died to themselves, to the world, and to their sinful natures. Coming up again, they were declared to have been raised with Christ to a new life. The themes of death and resurrection in baptism were dominant from the earliest days of the church (Rom. 6:4; Col. 2:12). Children watched from the banks of the river as men, women, and entire families boldly declared that they had died to their old way of life. They rose, dripping, to a new life. Words could hardly give a more accurate picture of the life-changing power of the gospel.

The Lord's Supper

Eating and drinking at the Lord's table gives believers, young and old, a full experience of the gospel. One not only hears the proclamation of God's saving love; one also sees, smells, tastes, and touches it.

"This is the body of Christ, broken for you."

"This is the blood of Christ, poured out for you."

Not only do the bread and wine speak to us of a bloody, broken sacrifice; they also speak of spiritual nourishment. They are food for the soul. Though denominations disagree on the exact meaning of Christ's presence in the bread and wine, we can all agree with Justin Martyr (A.D. 150) that these are not "common food and common drink."

Bread and wine are among the most powerful symbols of the Christian church. The mystery that they represent is sure to raise questions from children. And these questions in turn are sure to stimulate adults to rethink this mystery and its meaning in their own lives and situations.

Other Christian Symbols

The cross has become a symbol of God's justice and love intertwined. As children in the early church heard the story of Christ's death repeated throughout the church year, they began to see the cross as the central symbol of the gospel. The cross communicated pain and suffering as well as hope and mercy. As such, its meaning grew as children moved into the sometimes harsh reality of adulthood. It stood as a sign of a suffering God, one who poured himself out completely because he loved all people. It stood for the power in God's "weakness" and the wisdom in his "foolishness." The symbol of the cross called children and adults alike to expect suffering as they followed Jesus, their Lord.

Incense, another symbol in the worship of the early church, signified the prayers of God's people (Rev. 5:8; 8:3–4). Common in Jewish worship (Ex. 30:1), its use continued in the early church and still lives on in the Roman Catholic and Eastern Orthodox branches of the Christian church today. The sweet, pungent smell of burning incense was a vivid reminder that God indeed heard the prayers of his people. The wordless message of the incense prayer came to God as a sweet perfume, pleasing and impossible to ignore.

Candles, or the symbol of light, spoke of Christ's presence among the people gathered for worship. In Old Testament times, fire was a symbol of God's presence: the Sabbath lamp, the golden lampstand that stood in the Holy Place of the Temple, the pillar of fire that led Israel in the desert—these all pointed to the one who would say, "I am the light of the world." Many churches today light a Christ candle during each worship service because of the power of this imagery, allowing the small flame to speak a language without words.

The palm branches that children and adults have waved on Palm Sunday from the first century on also speak a language without words, an unspoken "Hallelujah!" to welcome the King riding on a donkey (the donkey is also a wordless symbol of Christ, proclaiming his humility and the nature of his servant-kingship).

The church has always recognized the images and symbols that speak to us of Jesus: the vine, the Way, the pearl of great price, bread, living water, a lamb, a lion, the King, a shepherd, the Word, the cornerstone, the morning star. These have been reproduced in art throughout the centuries, capturing the imagination of children as well as adults, drawing out their questions, becoming meaningful elements of their worship.

Summary

In both the Old and New Testaments, children grew in the worship and knowledge of God by being included in the rituals of family and public worship. They were confronted by symbols, by ordinary things turned extraordinary, by signs and actions that they didn't understand. They asked questions. Their curiosity was God's most effective tool of education—for both children and adults.

The adults, you see, learned too. Children's questions are often not easy to answer. They require careful thought, honesty, and clarity. Adults from the time of Abraham to the early church fathers must have despaired at the endless questions that came from the very young. But they also learned to rephrase their experience of God in words that made sense for their day, in words that a child could understand.

SUGGESTIONS FOR GROUP SESSION

Opening

Open your session by reading Psalm 78:1–7.

For Discussion

1. Think about your own family times together. Acknowledge that it's difficult, especially with busy schedules, to find a time for family devotions, for daily rituals and teaching or sharing. But children's questions provide a natural time to talk about God, about Bible stories, about worship and spiritual growth. When do your chil-

dren ask questions? What has prompted those questions? A story? A weekly routine? An unusual command or request from parents? What made you ask questions of your parents when you were a child?

Once you've listed a number of occasions that have prompted your children's (or your own) questions, brainstorm as a group to find ways to build these question-asking times into your family life. What can you do to stimulate your children's curiosity? What rituals or stories can you weave into your life as a family? Try to come up with a dozen or so suggestions; resolve to take one home and try it during the coming week.

2. This session mentions rituals and symbols in the life of the Old Testament Jewish family. Many of these were given by God to help Israel become a nation "set apart" from its neighbors. The Jew's goal was to stand apart from other cultures. We see this still today—the Hasidic Jews and the Amish are two examples of religious sects that have chosen to separate themselves by wearing clothes and living lifestyles that symbolize their distinctness from the world around them.

Is this a goal of ours today? Should it be? Is this feeling of being "set apart" something we want to instill in our children? How might the daily rituals of family life and the church accomplish this? What are the dangers of this separation? What positive things might result?

3. What are the basic things we want our children to learn about God and our relationship to him? How can we develop our *own* rituals and our *own* symbols (things that speak without words) to teach these to our children in our families?

4. What rituals and visual reminders in your church service and sanctuary serve to stimulate your children's questions? If a newcomer were to enter your service, what questions would he or she be likely to ask about the way you do things? What "visual aids," if any, have stirred your imagination and drawn you into worship?

5. Heidelberg Catechism Q & A 98 reads:

Q. But may not images be permitted in the churches as teaching aids for the unlearned?
A. No, we shouldn't try to be wiser than God.
   He wants his people instructed
      by the living preaching of his Word—
      not by idols that cannot even talk.

What difference do you see between using images—something the catechism warns against—and using symbols, signs, and rituals to call us to remember God's mighty acts and to lead us to worship him?

Closing

This session assumes that the process of children being formed spiritually by asking questions and receiving thoughtful answers is a good one. It also assumes that we adults have much to learn from this question/answer process.

Reflect for a moment on whether that assumption is really true in our society and in our homes today. Do we value and encourage our children's questions in the same way God's Old Testament people did? What might our children conclude by the way we typically respond to their questions?

Close your time together with prayer, asking that God will give you hearts that encourage and ears that are ready to listen to the questions of our children.

WORSHIPING TOGETHER
AT HOME

Dear God,
   I read that home is where God (that's you) is.
   What does that mean, I wonder?
   Does it mean if I am at religious school I am not away from home?
   Do I have to be in our living room to be with you?
   Are you everywhere?
   I am not sure. I just know that you are in my heart.
             From home,
             David
             (age 12)

Dear God,
   Thank you for my parents, my sister Anita, and for my grandma and grandpa. They are all real warm and special. I forgive you for my brother Phil.
   I guess you didn't finish working on him.
             Sean
             (age 12)

God,

My father reads to me from your book all the time. I like times when he does.

The Joseph character is interesting.

> Love,
> Joe
> (age 10)

—*excerpts from David Heller's* Dear God *(Doubleday, 1987)*

We may find these letters to God amusing; but if we look closer, they also tell us how central the home is in forming children's ideas of God.

Twelve-year-old David's letter reflects a warmth and an understanding of the word *home* that is unusual for his age, and he applies it to his budding relationship with God. Sean obviously loves his family, though he's not too sure about his pesky brother, Phil. (But even Phil finds grace in God's eyes, Sean seems to suggest.) Joe hears stories about God from his father, stories that pique his curiosity and foster his sense of closeness to God.

This session focuses on the home as the place where children learn the language and spirit of worship. You'll find lots of suggestions for family worship—ideas, liturgies, special celebrations, prayers. But first let's look at something even more essential for worshiping together at home—a warm and open atmosphere.

Foundations for Family Worship

I recently read an intriguing book entitled *The Dangers of Growing Up in a Christian Home* by Donald E. Sloat, Ph.D. (Thomas Nelson Publishers, 1986). The author, a practicing psychologist, has found a disturbing number of adults who are struggling with their relationship to God because of their upbringing in evangelical Christian homes. Here are a few of his insights:

> The way parents treat their children in daily living has more impact on their children's eventual spiritual development than the family's religious practices, including having family altar, reading the Bible together, attending church services, and so on.

> Perhaps you're wondering if I'm saying that regular family spiritual activities are not important. No, that's not my point. They are important, but the way parents treat their children in everyday living can subtly undermine all their lofty spiritual aspirations. When the children become adults with bitterness and resentment toward the church and their parents, the well-

intentioned parents are totally devastated and mystified. I believe many evangelical parents . . . have good intentions and positive spiritual goals for their children. In their minds they have followed worthy objectives without realizing that Christian principles can be undermined by poor relationships within the family. (81–82)

Though this may seem a negative way to start a lesson on family worship, it's important to realize that a regular time of family worship is not a magical guarantee of your children's spiritual health and growth.

Briefly, there are at least four foundations for worship in the home: *love, trust, freedom,* and *involvement.*

Love

Before family worship activities will have meaning for children, the home must be filled with love. Why? Because faith is a response to love, not merely an intellectual activity. (This is especially true of young children, who first learn about God through the love of parents who care for them.) Love is the heartbeat of faith.

Many parents, of course, believe in creating a loving home and in teaching their children about God. The problem lies in how to integrate the two. Sometimes we neglect to teach that God *is* love; rather, we teach a God who is overbearing, guilt-inducing, and solemn. We need to learn to express love in the context of our religious beliefs.

But, as Sloat says above, daily affection and genuine respect for each other matters above all. Worship in the home is the spiritual atmosphere created through everyday parenting. Family worship is most effective when parents use religious and family rituals to express love for their children.

This may sound intimidating and idealistic. It isn't meant to. You don't have to have a perfect home—just a lively, comfortable place where children feel free to ask questions and explore new ideas, secure in your love and respect for them.

Trust

As you recall from Session 2, a child's basic attitude of trust toward the world is established between infancy and age two. It is the foundation of one's approach to life and to God.

Along with love, there's no substitute for trust between parent and child. Unfortunately, trust grows only with diligent effort and purpose; mistrust comes more easily, by thoughtlessness and inattention.

Trust goes hand in hand with love. If your children trust you (and their brothers and sisters) not to laugh at their ideas, not to talk down to them, not to ignore their feelings, then they will participate much more freely in family worship.

Freedom

Children must feel free to ask questions and explore new ideas. This can be uncomfortable to Christian parents, who often feel happiest when their children have learned to use the right words to express their faith.

Something in every parent wants to take control, to discourage "heretical" ideas or questions from children. As a result, we hurry to supply rigid definitions instead of allowing our children some freedom to explore the limits and wonder of their faith. As a result, children can become either overly tentative about religious ideas or ardent in parroting their parents' faith, reciting "beliefs" that mean little to them. A parent's guidance, crucial to a child's spiritual growth, needs always to strike a balance between communicating the boundaries of God's law and giving the child freedom to explore God's truth and make it relate personally.

Involvement

With our busy lifestyles, this quality cannot be emphasized enough. There is no substitute for the parental investments of time, energy, caring, and personal sharing in the lives of their children.

Being involved means worshiping at home, not simply relying on the church to supply the primary worship experience for our children. As we saw in the previous session, God has chosen the family as the primary place to nurture children in the faith.

Given these foundations of family worship, let's look at some practical suggestions for the "family altar."

Whatever Happened to Table Devotions?

Many adults who grew up in the Reformed tradition recall the family meal as the time when everyone gathered for prayer and Bible reading. The formula was pretty standard: prayer before the meal, Bible reading (usually a chapter at a time) and prayer again after the meal. Here are one person's recollections:

> In the beginning was the Word. Every morning and evening I heard the Word. My father's voice would gravely read it at breakfast, after all of us had eaten and were eager to get ready for school. Only my father's strong will held us at the table.

Again my father read after dinner, when we all would sit, head in hands, thinking of other things until the interminable chapter of Leviticus or Jeremiah was finished.

He would read from Genesis to Revelation, one chapter per meal, and then start with Genesis all over again. We began to wait for our favorite stories—the ones not taught in school, like the Israelite who chopped up his fiancé and sent the parts of her body to the entire nation of Israel, or the beautiful Abishag who curled up in David's bed to keep the old king warm, or the axehead that floated mysteriously on the water. There was special delight when my father would read, in a strong and dignified voice, the phrase "him that pisseth against the wall."

The New Testament stories were not as interesting as the Old Testament ones, though they provided a welcome break between the long-winded prophets and the unfathomable epistles. Jesus didn't come alive for me in those stories the way the Old Testament heroes did. We weren't allowed to do much wondering about Jesus. He was God, so we couldn't really picture him scared when he was at the Temple at age twelve, or crying when he was young, or angry at his disciples. My father carefully explained that the Word was silent here. It didn't tell how Jesus felt. Besides, we weren't supposed to project our own feelings onto God.

God as Jesus never meant much to me—he didn't seem quite flesh-and-blood human. But God as Father—there was something to that. God had my own father's high seriousness, of course. God had a stern exterior, but one could always trust the softening of the eye, the unsanctified delight in a good glass of wine, the wink of the eye in a joke. God was not stuffy.

And God loved his children, though he was not above spanking them from time to time. I had felt my own father's hand on my backside often enough to know that.

Children learn about God through the nuances of family life. Family worship and prayer are important elements of those nuances. What tone of voice do parents use when they pray to or talk about God? Do the words "God" and "Jesus" turn up only in prayer and Bible reading, or do they appear naturally in everyday conversation? Is the atmosphere at family devotions one of freedom or control?

If children experience support and warmth in the home, what they learn there about God will take root. Often it will grow into healthy, genuine faith and worship. (Not always, unfortunately, as some parents have painfully learned.) Family worship can invite children to experience the everyday reality of a God who loves them, who hears their prayers, and who becomes tangible in the affection and respect they show to each other.

What are some ways to make table devotions, or the "family altar," more alive and enjoyable for your child? Much, of course, depends on the ages of the children in your family. If the oldest is two or three, mealtimes may be a test of endurance and grace. You may have to find simple bedtime rituals or times throughout the day when you say simple prayers or read a children's Bible story book together.

If your two-year-old has older brothers and sisters, however, he or she may be able to follow their example in sitting quietly, praying as a family, holding hands, lighting the candle (with help), and so on. From the age of four or five, most children are ready and eager for special family rituals and symbols that lead them into worship.

Based on the Old Testament model, the following suggestions emphasize the elements of family ritual and symbol. Drawn from a variety of resources and the experiences of several families, they are meant as suggestions to spark your own ideas, to help you create the rituals and symbols that will best nurture the spiritual life of your own family.

Bible stories, of course, are one of the most important elements of teaching children about God. There's nothing like a story to engage a child's imagination. Well-written Bible stories that are geared to your child's age level are excellent to read around the table or at bedtime. (Several good books for young children are *The Bible in Pictures for Little Eyes* by Kenneth N. Taylor, *Bible Stories for Children* by Geoffrey Horn and Arthur Cavanaugh, and *Story Bible for Young Children* by Anne DeVries.) If you like to read from the Bible for this family time, consider using the *International Children's Bible*, an excellent translation for children at a third-grade reading level. Or, if you're familiar enough with a particular Bible story, tell it in your own words. This will give the story a whole different flavor to your listeners.

Don't forget to tell your own stories, however. Just as the Israelites told and retold the stories of God's mighty acts to their children, so we are to tell our children our own faith stories and the stories of our parents and grandparents.

These stories, though they may seem a bit trivial or mundane to you (after all, who of us can claim the experiences of a Moses or Sarah?), may have a profound influence on your children's awareness of God. If you don't think you have any stories worth telling, think about these questions: When were you first aware of the reality of God? What made that happen? What did that feel like?

What were you thinking? What rituals in your family taught you about Jesus or the Father? What were your favorite Bible stories, and why? When do you first remember receiving an answer for something you prayed about? What doubts and questions did you have as a child? Were there any times when you felt especially close to God? What were they? How does knowing God make a difference in your life today?

> When I was very young, about five or six years old, one of the kittens that played outside our house was killed, run over by a car. I ran to rescue the little body, which looked still intact and whole. The kitten was dead, but I decided there and then that God could make it alive again. All it needed was a little prayer and faith.

> I prayed the rest of that morning, sitting at the edge of our house, stroking the kitten and telling God I was sure he could bring it back to life. I looked at its body, so soft and broken, and I cried and prayed. Nothing changed.

> Finally, at the end of the morning, I was faced with a choice. Either God didn't really have the power to make things alive again, or else he simply chose not to, for reasons I couldn't understand. After thinking for a bit, I decided that God loved the kitten as much as I did, but that he simply didn't agree with what I was asking for. I trusted that God had his reasons. I let my brother bury the kitten.

This story tells of a child's experience with death, grief, trust, and the mystery of prayer. I suspect my children would love to hear it. But I've never told it to them. Why? I'm not sure. It never really seemed important until I retold it here.

You may also have stories that you've never thought of telling. Tell them in your family devotional time. You may be surprised at how many questions they will bring out from your children, like the stories of the Israelites long ago. To paraphrase Joshua 4:6— (from the story of the twelve stones), "In the future, when your children ask you, 'What do these stones mean?' tell them . . . These stones will be a memorial to your children forever."

But the children won't be the only ones who benefit. These stories will also take on new meaning for you. (You may want to actually gather a collection of family stones, each one representing an important point in your family's life. Paint on each stone a word or two that reminds you of that time.)

Sometimes others' stories are also a good vehicle for the gospel and a way to introduce family discussion and worship. Two such storybooks are David and Karen Mains's *Tales of the Kingdom* and

Tales of the Resistance (both published by David C. Cook, 1983 and 1986). These are tales of the struggle between good and evil and the mystery of God's kingdom. You may want to read these aloud, or purchase them on cassette tape and listen to them as a family. Even young children can appreciate them, though the language is geared to older children.

Also helpful for family worship are the stories and devotionals by James Schaap: *Intermission, Someone's Singing, Lord*, and *No Kidding, God*, published by CRC Publications.

Basic to family worship is a time for praying together. Mealtimes and bedtimes seem to be the easiest times of day to establish regular prayer. Family prayer does not have to be a formal affair. Hold hands during prayer. Ask one child to open or close the meal with prayer, or open it up to sentence prayers from the whole family. Or, better yet, use this time to share together the most important event of each individual's day or week. After you're done talking, simply thank God together for the good things that happened.

Try hard not to make your children feel like their prayers are a performance to be evaluated. There is a subtle difference between saying "I really appreciated your prayer" and "Boy, was that a great prayer you just said!" Many parents are performance- and praise-oriented (and that can be good), and these comments slip out easily, giving children the impression that they're praying to (or for) their parents, not to God. Such comments can also leave the impression that words make a good prayer, rather than the attitude of one's heart.

Remember also to include times of praise, of simply worshiping God for who he is. Read a psalm together (Psalm 89 or 103 are eloquent songs of praise) to "warm up" for your own sentence prayers or silent time of praising God. Use prayers from other sources too, and invite each family member to say or read a line (See CLOSING at the end of this session for an example). Or write your own prayers as a family, with each person adding lines that express who God is. You might use such prayers regularly, weaving them into your family rituals—especially on holy days like Christmas, Easter, and Pentecost.

During these family prayers, consider using symbols to draw your children into worship. Lighting a Christ candle is one way to visibly remind even the smallest child that Jesus is present and that his presence brings light into the dark and troubled places of our lives. Involve the children in this ritual by allowing them to light and snuff the candle (you may find a candle-snuffer helpful). Don't forget to take time simply to enjoy the light of the Christ candle and let its meaning take root in your imaginations.

(Some children may feel sad when the flame is snuffed out,

thinking it means that Christ is no longer present. You'll want to explain that just as the smoke rises and filters through the room unseen, so Christ's presence is always with us.)

A prayer list is another visual reminder of the concerns your family is praying for. For children who can't read yet, you might make a list that includes photographs of family members and missionaries to pray for, along with other pictures to represent more general concerns. Your children may want to draw some of the pictures themselves. Instead of a list, you could put each request or picture on a 3" x 5" card; distribute them at prayer time so that each family member can choose one or two to pray for. You might leave a basket on the table in which children can put new prayer requests as they think about them.

If your children are old enough to be busy in sports, music lessons, and other after-school activities, your family schedule may be hectic! If so, try setting aside one night each week for your special family dinner. Make it a celebration; use candles, the good dishes, the fancy silverware. Include your time of sharing and family prayer, along with other worship rituals you may have developed over the years.

Other Prayer Times

Bedtime rituals of prayer can become warm, memorable times. Again, how you do these rituals and prayers is often more important than what you say during them. Alyce Oosterhuis, assistant professor of education at The King's College in Edmonton, Alberta, shares these reflections:

> I would not want my children to fear, obey, and respect God any less than I do or did as a child. But in reflecting on the way we pray, I have changed many of their childhood rituals to teach them that God is primarily a parent who loves, who understands our stumblings, who can laugh as well as cry, who is ever present in all that we do.

> The bedtime rituals of prayer before sleep have become very special parent-child moments in our family life. We hug each other during prayer time (God's love surrounds us). We tell God about the day's events and tomorrow's hopes (God is vitally involved in all that we do). Sometimes we giggle during prayer (God is a God of laughter). Occasionally we take turns praying (God appreciates children's words no less than adults').

Does your home have a quiet, private place where family members can go to be alone and to pray? Most homes don't have an empty room to spare, but you might consider setting up a folding screen and an old chair in a room that is not used often—the basement, perhaps. Also include a Bible, a candle, and other symbols that speak of God's love to you and your children. Your children may not use it often, but they will see the adults use it from time to time and know that prayer is an important part of their lives. Just the presence of such a place in your house speaks without words, giving worship and prayer a place alongside of eating, sleeping, watching TV, and so on.

Regular times for prayer are good, but they should not replace the opportunities that walk in your door when children come home from school or from a friend's home with problems, hurt feelings, insecurities, or broken friendships. Blending hugs, reassurance, sharing, and prayer together at these times makes family worship a more meaningful and natural part of the family's life.

Other Worship Activities

Music played a large role in the worship of the Old Testament Israelites. Most of their songs have been preserved for us in the book of Psalms. Music is still a major part of public Christian worship today. However, it seems to have largely died out of family worship.

This unfortunate loss can be quickly remedied, however, especially in families with young children, by making or purchasing simple musical and rhythm instruments. Tambourines, blocks, finger cymbals, chimes, bells, simple xylophones, paper plates stapled together with beans inside—children love to play these to accompany simple choruses and lively hymns. Use these along with records and tapes of music as well. If any family member plays a "regular" instrument, find ways to include that talent in your worship from time to time—especially for Christmas and Easter songs. Singing and making music together adds liveliness and a sense of fun to family worship times.

For young children, perhaps the hardest part of any worship—family or church—is having to sit quietly and not disturb others. You can combine your child's energy and curiosity with family worship by taking a nature walk once a week or with the change of every season, discovering the fascinating and varied parts of God's creation. Help your young children gather leaves, twigs, stones, feathers, insects, and bring them home to be part of your family worship. As part of your devotions, talk about the amazing creativity and power of the God who made them. Make this part of your "thank you" list to God. Young children will feel good that their discoveries have contributed to the family time, and adults will gain a new appreciation for seeing God's world through a child's eyes.

Another way to make devotions come alive in the imaginations of your children is to check out books from the library that retell the story you're reading in family devotions or Sunday school. Or find books that expand on elements of the story (angels, donkey, shepherds, light, salt, and so on) and read these during the week.

Special Family Occasions

Birthdays are wonderful occasions for special worship around the table, a time of thanksgiving and appreciation for the person whose birth you are celebrating. Robert Webber's *The Book of Family Prayer* (available through Worship Resources, 219 W. Franklin, Wheaton, IL 60187) includes a short, simple birthday liturgy that family members can participate in.

Remembering the date of a child's baptism is also a way to deepen its meaning for your family. Some churches give small banners, certificates, candles, or other mementos at baptism. Save these and bring them out each year as a memorial to one of the most important events of your child's spiritual life.

Births and deaths in the family are times when your worship together can focus on Scriptures that speak of these themes, of the life that God created within us and the certainty of death that comes to everyone. Encourage your children to ask questions and to express their feelings and fears and thoughts to God as well as to you. Read Scripture passages that speak of the hope of the resurrection and of the new bodies that we will be given (1 Corinthians 15, for example). Remind the children of the specialness of their own birth and read together portions of Psalm 139. You might conclude your worship with a simple liturgy that the children can easily memorize, like this ancient prayer, spoken with cupped hands:

> Lord of day and night,
>   of life and death,
> we place ourselves
>   and our concerns
>   into your holy hands. Amen.

(This prayer can also be used after your family has talked about the concerns on your prayer list. Rather than mentioning all of these again in prayer, simply lift them up to God with these simple words.)

Note: Celebrating the church liturgical year with children brings many more opportunities for creative family worship. These suggestions are presented in Session 6. (For some additional ideas in family worship, see *Reformed Worship* 12, a special issue on children in worship. Available from CRC Publications.)

Making Time in a Busy Schedule

After reading this session, some of us may feel motivated, excited, and ready to try some new ways of worshiping with our families. Others may feel frustrated and discouraged. Already our days are too full, or our time and energy is depleted by active and demanding children. Trying to find creative ways to lead our children into worship may seem like the icing on the cake—or like the straw that broke the camel's back.

To this I can only say that I have been there. There are no easy answers to the problem of days that are too short and commitments or interruptions that seem endless.

On the other hand, God did not intend that we live like that—with little time for family worship, for reflection, for spiritual refreshment, for quiet and peace. The small seed of God's word in our souls gets choked out by other cares and concerns. We suffer and our children suffer. I believe that God also suffers.

There are two things that I have found helpful in this area of family worship. First, it is imperative to set aside some time each day to remember who I am and for what purpose I am alive. "Remember . . . remember . . . remember," calls the Lord to his people all the way through the Old Testament. "Never forget the love of the Lord your God."

For me, remembering means rising a little earlier, carving out five or ten or fifteen minutes to be silent and alone. Though this early morning silence is sometimes crowded out, for weeks or even months at a time, I have found out that I can always come back to it.

On days when I conclude my "remembering time" only to be greeted by fights, spilled juice, tears, and broken dishes, I may still find myself yelling at the top of my voice. "Mom's really lost it this time," I overheard my daughter say, very quietly, during the last outbreak two days ago. But the good thing is that the images and thoughts from the early morning quietness help me to remember my life, to put it back together again, to restore peace within myself and my family.

These symbols and stories are the seeds of God's word in my life. They subtly change my perspective, so that gradually nothing seems more important than that my family know God. Out of that conviction comes the energy and the creativity to make family worship a vital part of our life together.

Second, it's important to realize that family worship activities are not something we do *for* our children but *with* our children. We have much to offer them and they have much to offer us. In the midst of this group of people that we call family, we seek the mystery of the secret of our lives. Our children need our stories, our wealth of accumulated experiences, our modeling of God's trustworthy and loving character. We need their curiosity, their questions, their impatience with shallow answers, their capacity for trust and warmth and love.

We need each other to find God and to worship Him. Our family worship times can help us do that. Our worship times help us best when they are planned to include every member and when they reflect the love and trust that is already present in our homes.

SUGGESTIONS FOR GROUP SESSION

Opening

Distribute pens and paper and take five minutes to jot down your responses to the following:

Think back on your childhood family devotions, if that was part of your growing up. What do you remember most about those times? What was the mood? Who led them, and what did that person do? Aside from the spoken words, what was communicated (in tone of voice, in the rituals established, in the things that were prayed about, in the choice of what was read, and so on)?

Spend a few minutes talking about the experiences you've recorded. What did you learn from these times that you carry with you still today? What is there in those memories that you wish to bring into your own family life today? Why is it important to you?

For Discussion

1. Our lives are full of stories—people, events, funny things, sad things, memories. God is present in all of those stories, as he is present in all of life. Once we begin to tell our stories, we realize his presence in them because of the insights they bring, the life that comes into our voices as we speak, the interest and curiosity in our children's eyes as they listen.

   Think back on the years of your childhood and growing up. What events—pleasant or painful—changed your life? What brought you to the awareness of God in your life? Take a few minutes to jot down on a piece of paper one or two stories that come back to you. Then share one with the group, if you can. As a group, make a commitment to share at least one of these stories with your immediate family during the coming week.

2. What has been your greatest obstacle in establishing regular family worship times? Make a list of these obstacles in your

group. Don't suggest solutions or answers. Try instead to help each other get to the root of what the obstacles really are.

Then take the time to pray together, perhaps in pairs or small groups, asking God to show you ways to overcome these obstacles. After prayer, spend about five minutes in silence, writing down solutions you think God might offer for your own situation. Share these with the group, if people feel free enough to do so.

3. The session mentioned using a lit candle and a prayer list as two visual symbols in your family worship time. Can you think of any other visual reminders of God's presence to use during this time? What things would be helpful for your particular family? For other families in general? What might be some good symbols to include with specific Bible stories or parables, especially with young children?

4. The session also mentions some resources that might be helpful in making family worship livelier and more meaningful for children. As a group, add to that list by sharing with each other some that you are familiar with and have used successfully. (You might want to take your favorites to this session and pass them around for a closer look.) Perhaps a volunteer from the group can compile a master list and duplicate it for all to use.

Closing

Use the following prayer from *I, Francis* by Carlo Carretto to close your session today. Read it in unison or take turns, each group member reading a line. (If you use this prayer at home, as suggested earlier in this session, be sure to take the opportunity it provides to talk with your children about words like "omnipotent," "eternal," "meekness," "security," and so on.)

You alone are holy, Lord God, Worker of Wonders.
You are mighty.
You are great.
You are the Most High.
You are omnipotent, our holy Father, King of heaven and earth.
You, Lord God, three and one, are our every good.
You, Lord God, all good, our highest good—Lord God living and true.
You are charity and love.
You are wisdom.
You are humility.
You are patience.
You are security.
You are peace.

You are joy and gladness.
You are justice and temperance.
You are riches altogether sufficient.
You are beauty.
You are meekness.
You are our protector.
You are our strength.
You are our refreshment.
You are our hope.
You are our faith.
You are our most profound sweetness.
You are our eternal life, great and admirable Lord,
omnipotent God, merciful Savior!

WORSHIPING TOGETHER AT
CHURCH

Dear God,
Do your kids watch cartoons on Saturdays? Or are they helping you get ready for church on Sunday?
Your friend,
Ted (age 7)

Dear God,
Can't you make church more fun? What about having a few videos?
Just trying to help,
Celia (age 10)

Dear God,
At church my minister talks a lot about throwing stones and sins. Any idea what he means?
I think you must know. I don't get the hang of this stuff.
A regular church-goer,
Artie (age 11)

—*excerpts from David Heller's* Dear God *(Doubleday, 1987)*

Children and church. At best, they seem to mix like oil and water. At worst, they mix like nitric and hydrochloric acid. One seven-year-old I know very personally has exploded a number of times from the pressure of having to conform to his mother's whispered commands: "Sit still!" "Stop that!" "Get *away* from your sister!"

Such explosions come because many Sunday worship services are designed to leave children out. Theological language, as we've noted in earlier sessions, is full of difficult concepts: omnipotence, grace, salvation, atonement, justification, and so on. The words of hymns, the invocation, the prayers, and the sermon are usually on a high-school reading level. Thus we have worship services which focus primarily on speaking and listening and minimally on right-brain activities (drama, movement, color, etc.). These services effectively shut out children from meaningful participation.

An even greater barrier to including children in worship, of course, is the assumption that children have nothing to offer. Many of us assume—perhaps because we've never thought much about it—that children are there simply to learn. We take them along so that someday, when they grow up, they'll be able to worship like we do.

Do our worship services say "Wait till you're an adult—then you can *really* worship"? Do we unknowingly keep our children at arm's length from Jesus? If so, for what reasons? I suspect the reasons are much like those of the well-intentioned disciples who discouraged parents from bringing their children to be touched and blessed by Jesus. "That's all very nice, of course," they told the parents, "but Jesus is busy with important, adult matters right now. We're talking *kingdom* work here. Maybe another time, when his schedule is lighter."

What does our worship say about the place of children in the kingdom? Perhaps our services say something that we don't really want or intend to say. Our theology, after all, goes out of its way to promote infant baptism.

Baptism—of children as well as adults—says, "Welcome! You belong to our family, in the name of Christ! You are part of God's covenant now, and we will do everything in our power to include you in the family of God . . . (except during the worship service, of course. There we will ask you to sit very quietly and not bother us while we talk about things you can't understand yet and do things that you can't be a part of until you're older, like us)."

None of us would add that last part, of course. But look at the way we worship with our children. When we gather as a congregation, do we "receive these children in love, pray for them, help instruct them in the faith, and encourage and sustain them in the fellowship of believers"? Or do we try to keep them as quiet and unnoticed as possible?

The nature of Christian worship calls us to include children because it calls us to include *everyone*. Weak and strong, rich and poor, old and young—all are welcome and important in the kingdom. Worship is to reflect that sense of welcome and equality.

Worship is also inclusive in that it is not a spectator event. Each person who enters the sanctuary is called to bring all of himself or herself to worship. Have we become accustomed to watching a few people "perform" while we sit quietly and think our private thoughts? Have we forgotten Paul's description of worship: "When you come together, everyone has a hymn, or a word of instruction, a revelation, a tongue or an interpretation" (1 Cor. 14:26)?

The goal of worship is not to put on an impressive pageant, performed flawlessly. *The goal of worship is to praise, glorify, and adore our God.* God's family gathers, adults and children alike, to bring a gift or a song or a prayer to share in worship. To exclude anyone goes against the inclusive nature of Christian worship.

The nature of children also compels us to include them in worship. What is it about children that made Jesus present them as examples of what it means to receive the kingdom of God?

First, children know that they are dependent on others for survival—and they are not ashamed of it. Most children live with parents who are loving providers. When children need something, all they need to do is ask for it.

We adults, on the other hand, tend to forget the one without whom we could not take a single breath. We forget the one by whose power the universe—and the stock market—holds together. We need the presence of children among us in worship to remind us that we too are dependent children of a loving Parent.

Second, children also teach us openness and exuberance in loving. Toddlers wander up to adults, touch them, gaze without guile into their eyes, and smile. Young children fling their arms around us and plant kisses on our faces with enthusiasm. They shamelessly seek and give affection. They love us without criticism. Their friendship is without deception, their love is without hidden motives.

Giving children a chance to model this love in our worship services—an uncritical, trusting, generous, and affectionate openness to others and to God—also gives adults a powerful object lesson on the kingdom of God and on the atmosphere of Christian worship.

Jesus may also have had in mind the spontaneity and exuberance that children show when they're enjoying something. They cannot help but show their enthusiasm.

Once when I was young, I waved my handkerchief madly at the minister as he walked by our pew. He was a gentle and godly man with snow-white hair, and I waved at him to show my affection and pleasure at seeing him. My mother snatched away my handkerchief, of course, and firmly put my hand down by my side. I learned that behaving in church means not doing anything spontaneous or exuberant. (I would probably, without thinking, do the same thing today to my own children. But another part of me would wish that the adults were free enough to wave their handkerchiefs too.)

For many adults, honor and respect for God in worship entails a quiet, passive stillness, inactive and calm. Spontaneity and exuberance don't fit this expectation. Children who wiggle, squirm, and are sometimes loud and enthusiastic do not seem worshipful or reverent. But if respectful worship can also include a delighted, joyful, grateful, heartfelt response to God, then children are fully qualified to take part. In fact, they may model true Christian worship for more reticent adults.

Quietness and stillness have their place in worship, of course—and children are capable of sensing this too. But exuberance and spontaneity also belong. Long ago, David danced before the Lord—today he might be thrown out of the sanctuary!

One more quality that children bring to worship: the need for color, movement, texture, story, drama, dance, symbol. Responding to this need will also enrich our experience of worship and give us new ways to express our feelings toward God. Along with children, we will find our imaginations fired, our minds stimulated, our hearts stirred to praise the living God. And that's what worship is all about!

Where Can We Start?

At this point, some of us will be ready to go full-steam ahead, ready to talk about specific ways of including children in our worship. Others may feel like drawing back, voicing questions such as: What specific changes are we talking about here? Are we opening the door to pandemonium? How will including children affect our usual way of worshiping?

These concerns are legitimate. Children being who they are, some structure and order is necessary as a balance to all that energetic curiosity and enthusiasm. Children respond best to structure when they understand why it's there.

Education, therefore, is one of the first steps to including children in our worship. Knowing the different parts of the liturgy, for example, or the meaning of the sacraments, or how to use a hymnbook—these are basic to a child's participation in worship.

Many churches have assumed that this education about worship happens by osmosis. They reason that children will absorb this knowledge after ten or twelve years of sitting in the pew. Unfortunately, this produces a generation of adults who don't understand the flow of the liturgy, the meaning of the symbols, and the theology behind it all. They cling to the traditional way of doing things simply "because that's the way we've always done it."

If we intentionally educate our children about worship, however, we will produce not only a generation but also an entire congregation alive to the spirit of its worship liturgy. We'll not be afraid of changes that truly enhance worship—and we'll know what things not to throw away.

When we educate our children about worship, we should teach at least the following:

- The conviction that everyone—young and old—can actively participate in worship
- The purpose of the furniture and the symbols in the sanctuary
- The roles of different people who lead in worship
- The meaning of the various parts of the liturgy
- The relationship between the Scripture that is read, the sermon, and the songs
- A familiarity with the creeds of the church, the Gloria Patri, and the doxology
- The meaning of difficult words in worship: holy, alleluia, praise, confess, and so on
- How to use the hymnal
- The meaning of the sacraments
- How a worship service is prepared and put together

This instruction, of course, should not simply *tell* children about worship. We must help them experience, touch, hear, and see the things we talk about—let them dip their fingers in the baptismal font, teach them to sing the doxology, help them find things in the hymnbook. If you're looking for good resources to use in such a course, consider *God's Children in Worship* (a course on worship for children and congregation, available from Discipleship Resources, P.O. Box 189, Nashville, TN 37202), and the book *Children in the Worshiping Community* by David Ng and Virginia Thomas (John Knox Press, 1981). Both offer excellent suggestions for teaching about worship, geared to the child's age level.

Suggestions for Including Children

It's no use teaching children about the elements of worship if they can't take an active part in the worship service. Children learn by doing, by experiencing. Then the spoken explanations begin to make sense.

Older children especially are ready to help in leading a portion of the service or planning segments of it. Younger children are delighted to have a part in some of the pageantry of worship, especially if assisted by their parents. Here are some suggestions for including children, starting roughly from the beginning of the service and ending with the benediction. Use them to spark your own ideas.

- If you have adult greeters, have them ask their children to stand with them to distribute the children's bulletins, greet newcomers' children, and so on.
- Many churches sing several songs of praise at the beginning of the service to "warm up" for worship. The minister or song leader could ask the children present if they have a favorite song they'd like to sing, either from the hymnal or from a collection of simple Bible songs that the congregation knows.
- Ask a different church education class each week to choose and practice a song that they think would be a good opening for worship. If it's a new song, ask them to help lead the congregation in singing it, along with the worship or song leader.
- If your church lights a Christ candle to symbolize the presence and light of Christ during the worship service, ask children to light the candle at the beginning of the service each week. Train them beforehand to use the candle lighter/snuffer, and make sure an adult stands by to help.
- Ask one of your church school classes to think about the qualities of God that they like the most. Put their ideas into the form of a prayer or a psalm of praise to use at the beginning of the service as a call to worship. (Ask a child from the class to read it, or have several read it antiphonally.) Print the prayer or psalm in the bulletin as well, and make sure the children know when it will be used during the service.
- Teach children simple liturgical dance movements to an opening hymn of praise and ask them to dance while the congregation sings. Invite adults who have learned the movements also to participate. The enjoyment and grace of dance should be open to old and young alike.
- Learn the opening hymn (or one of the other more simple hymns) as part of your worship time in the church education classes the previous Sunday. Talk about the theme of the song and the history behind it, if possible. Read the psalm or Scripture verse that is associated with it. Discuss the meaning of any difficult words that appear, and encourage the children to listen for the hymn during the service and to sing along as well as they can.
- After the children have learned the meaning of the time of confession and assurance of pardon, you might occasionally ask them (along with the rest of the congregation) to keep a list during the coming week of things they've done or said that may have displeased God or hurt other people. (Parents can help non-readers with their lists.) Ask members to bring their unsigned lists

as a letter of confession to the service the following Sunday. After a brief prayer of confession, allow a time of silence in which young and old can remember the specific sins they wrote down and silently ask God for forgiveness. Then collect the papers and put them in a trash bag as a visible reminder that believers can throw their "lists" away after they confess their sin.

This exercise helps children become more aware of things that may stand between us and God in worship. It also serves as a concrete lesson to all of us that God doesn't remember our sins after confession, and neither should we. After confession, we are free to worship!

- Ask children during the church education time to think of things that people might do or say that hurt their friendship with God and with other people. Write down their suggestions and use them in the time of confession during the service: "Forgive us, God, when we . . . " This will help make the prayer of confession more accessible and personal to the children.
- Ask children to read the Scripture occasionally, especially if you have various church members read the texts chosen for that Sunday in the lectionary. You will find good readers even as young as first and second grade. Be sure they have large print to read from, and ask their parents to practice with them beforehand.
- If the Scripture for the sermon is a story, use children and adults in a reader's theater presentation, rather than having the minister read it from the pulpit. (For more details on a reader's theater, see the discussion later in this lesson.)
- If your congregation is small enough, you may regularly ask for prayer requests before the congregational prayer. Encourage parents to be aware of needs their children may want prayed for (sick friends, problems at school, exam time) so that if the children are too shy to make the requests, the parents can do so. Or collect lists of concerns from the church education classes and include these in the congregational prayer. If the prayer time is opened up to the congregation so that members can pray for specific requests, encourage children to offer prayers also.
- Older children can help collect the offering and can pray the offertory prayer as well (let them know beforehand what cause the offering is going to support).
- Involve children as much as possible in the offering for the week. If they receive an allowance or have some source of income, encourage them to put their own money in the collection plate. To nurture "cheerful givers", it's important that children be sympathetic to the cause they're supporting. Take time to present it

clearly to the children before the offering, or tell the church education classes a week ahead of time so the children can raise money for it during the week. Encourage children who have no money to write (or have their parents write for them) a note of thanks or praise to God and to put it in the plate as it's passed. Emphasize that the spirit of giving something to God is more important than how much is given.

- Some churches use five or ten minutes after the sermon as a time when people can respond to what they've heard by singing familiar songs, offering simple prayers, or reading short passages of Scripture. This time not only gives the children an opportunity to offer a song or prayer but also teaches them that every member comes with something to offer in worship.
- Before an appropriate hymn, you can distribute (or have children come forward to choose) instruments to accompany the singing: tambourines, finger cymbals, blocks, triangles, bells, rhythm instruments, and so on. Have the children accompany the organ or piano, the voices, and whatever other instruments you may be using to "make a joyful noise to the Lord." Adults may want to join in with instruments (or jingling key rings) too.
- Involve children in music as much as possible—through children's choirs, bell choirs, solos, teaching the congregation the motions to a song, playing musical instruments along with the organ or piano accompaniment. Remember that the goal of worship is not a flawless performance but rather the joy of giving praise to God together.

As children grow more used to taking part in worship, consider including some as members of your worship team. Listen to what they feel is helpful in worship; follow through on ideas that seem valid in light of your theology of worship.

These suggestions just scratch the surface. The most important thing is the spirit of worship and inclusiveness that we communicate to the children among us.

Including Children at Sermon Time

The Mount Everest of worship, however, remains to be scaled: How do we keep young children involved and interested in a twenty- to thirty-minute sermon?

Some churches find it best to let the younger children (ages three to six) out of the sanctuary at this point for their own worship activities, geared to their needs and understanding. This is understandable, since sitting with preschoolers through a sermon can mean missing worship and Word altogether. Other congregations have set up a "crèche corner"—an area in the back of the sanctuary with carpeted benches, books, crayons and paper, soft dolls, and so on. The children are free to come here at certain points during the service to play quietly (rather than playing quietly in the pew), supervised by an adult. This way children are not separated from the worshiping congregation, yet also are not distracting the adults or confined to a hard pew.

An ideal goal, however, is to include children as much as possible during the sermon time. Here much of the work lies with the preacher. The following are some suggestions that may make a difference:

- Use stories whenever you can to teach biblical truths. Stories make things come alive. During even the most lucid logical argument or brilliant textual analysis, people's minds wander easily. But start to tell a story, and their ears are back in focus—especially the children's. Sharing your personal experiences, retelling favorite stories from childhood, or dramatizing a story from Scripture will spark your listeners' imaginations and draw out the "aha" of the spiritual truth you want to communicate.
- Appeal to your listeners' eyes as well as their ears. Use an overhead projector or a flip chart with markers to write down key words, phrases, and diagrams. Our seven-year-old, usually struck with boredom during the sermon, listened intently to a twenty-five-minute sermon on the Trinity simply because the pastor used a flip chart to write down questions and to draw the lines of relationship between Father, Son, and Spirit.
- Action helps too. If kids can't be active themselves, they like to watch action. Not too many ministers are free enough to mimic David's dancing in front of the ark, but one preacher tried it, and our kids never forgot that story and the sermon.
- Using all the senses—sight, smell, touch, and so on—makes for an unforgettable sermon. One pastor, preaching on prayer as sweet incense that rises to God's throne, lit a stick of incense to make his point. What a graphic reminder that God cannot ignore the prayers of the saints, any more than we can ignore the smell of incense filling the sanctuary.
- Finally, use simple language to talk about profound things. The Hebrew rabbis taught that even the deepest of God's truths could be clearly explained to a small child. If you use difficult words, explain them. Use word pictures as much as you can. Symbols, images, metaphors—these all can make theological terms like justification or sanctification come alive. This advice will also help the adult listener—especially the person unfamiliar with the church, who has to guess at the meaning of such common words as "grace" and "salvation."

Adding Color, Movement, and Symbol to Worship

Introducing more right-brain elements—color, texture, movement, story, and the like—into the service will also enable children to participate more fully in worship. Let's consider some of these in greater detail.

- Banners are one way of introducing color, texture, and visual symbols into the worship setting. Children's eyes are drawn to them, and their imaginations slowly take in the message spoken through the symbols, words, and colors.

  Kids are wonderful at designing and making banners too. The third-grade church education class made our Epiphany banner several years ago, and it was a splendid depiction of the gifts of the Magi with all the extravagance of childhood, full of glitter and jewels and fancy trim. The children's eyes lit up when their banner took its place at the front of church during Epiphany; they knew the meaning of each gift and the story behind the celebration.
- Other visual symbols are equally effective in "speaking without words" of the presence of God in worship. Some churches use a "Christ candle": a large, white candle that burns throughout the year and is traditionally replaced each Easter. The candle is lit at the beginning of the service and snuffed out after the benediction, signifying the presence of Christ among his people gathered for worship. It reminds us also that the light of the Word chases away the darkness of sin and death in our lives.
- The cross at the front of the sanctuary is of one of the most powerful symbols of our faith. Refer to it often in your services, explaining its meaning in different contexts to draw the children into the power of its imagery of God's love, of Jesus' suffering, of our salvation, and of the journey of the Christian life.
- The colors and symbols of the changing church seasons and holy days are also a powerful reminder of the stories of the Christian faith; they will be discussed in greater detail in the next lesson.
- Dance serves as another kind of symbol, a physical expression of our praise to God. Dance and praise were inextricably intertwined in Israel's worship, as Miriam and the women demonstrated after the Israelites' deliverance from Egypt. Dance allows us to express without words the emotions of worship. To children, dancing comes as naturally as hugging and skipping and stamping their feet—all ways they display their emotions in everyday life.

  We adults are more inhibited when it comes to dance; we've learned to limit our communication to words and simple gestures. Perhaps the children can teach us how to move our bodies again in praise and thanksgiving to God.

  Some churches have dance ministries that practice weekly and use their gifts in a highly orchestrated dance during the service. Others simply teach the children simple movements to familiar songs and invite them up to the front of the sanctuary once in while to dance with the singing. Either way, the medium of dance brings our songs to life.

Including Children Through Drama

Drama is another way of bringing words to life in our worship. Jesus' parables provide delightful scenes and dialogue for your church's budding actors, giving the very old and the very young an opportunity to work together on presenting the Word during the service. If a full-blown drama seems too much to handle, try a reader's theater, in which several people read the narrative while others pantomime the actions of the story.

The "here-and-now-ness" of drama makes it a highly effective way to present the Scriptures for the sermon. Seeing Ruth and Naomi clinging together on their way to Bethlehem, for example, is much more memorable than hearing the minister read, "So Naomi returned, and Ruth the Moabitess with her." Children will remember what they've seen, think about the emotions portrayed by the characters, and ask questions they wouldn't have thought of if the Scripture had been merely read.

Church education classes can work on putting together a reader's theater several weeks in advance. This gives them a chance to put themselves into the story, to wrestle with the meaning and with the emotions that lie behind the words, and to put their creative talents to good use. Letting them discover the main concepts of the story on their own helps them learn it on a deeper level than if you provide the meaning for them; it also allows them to share their insights with the rest of the congregation in the context of worship.

Using puppets is another way to involve children in presenting the Word or related stories. Whether children actually work puppets or simply observe them, puppets have a way of making content come alive in children's imaginations.

Other visual aids to worship are limited only by the scope of your imagination. On a mission emphasis Sunday, for example, create a visual feast by having a grand procession down the aisle, adults and children carrying the flags of countries in which your denomination supports missionaries. As they line up at the front, the flag carriers step forward as the name of each country is called out and a brief description of the mission to that country is read. It's a colorful, festive way to celebrate the mission work of the church.

If you are marking the anniversary of your church or working on a statement of your church's vision and goals, create a timeline of your church's history to display in the sanctuary for a few Sundays. List the events that have made you a family and that show God's continuing love and faithfulness to your congregation. Post pictures of people who have been important at different points in your history. As the Israelites of the Old Testament did, retell the faith stories of your members and make sure the children are in on the storytelling. Think of symbols for God's faithfulness that will draw out their questions. Make a heap of stones and pebbles in the sanctuary, with a member's name written on each one. The children will love this visual reminder that they are part of the "living stones" that make up the house of God.

Using the Sacraments as Signs and Symbols

Our sacramental worship liturgies include common, everyday elements that are essential ingredients of our life: water, bread, and wine. Used as religious symbols, they call to our imagination and bring us into a deeper reflection of all that God has done for us and in us. As Thomas Fawcett says in *The Symbolic Language of Religion*,

> A most important feature of symbols lies in their richness of expression. They have what Josiah Royce calls 'surplus of meaning,' the ability to speak of many things. . . . In fact, a true symbol appears to be always capable of new applications and evocative of new insights.

The sacraments of baptism and communion are two of the richest "visual aids" God has given the church. Baptism—a sign of washing, of burial, and of resurrection—is the mark of entrance into the kingdom. The Lord's Supper nurtures our spirits with its visual and physical reminder of pierced flesh and spilled blood that makes us whole.

Children in our tradition are already included in the rite of baptism, though they are usually too young to appreciate its meaning at the time. But each new baptism they witness as they grow up in God's family becomes an opportunity to impress the symbol of the cleansing water more deeply in their imaginations.

In a way, we somewhat limit the symbol of baptism when we sprinkle rather than immerse infants and adults who are being baptized. The few drops of water on the forehead don't really picture for us the complete cleansing, our burial with Christ, and our rising with him to a new life. One minister pours water over the top of the infant's head and lets some splash to the floor "so the children can see that we're really using water." Often children are invited up to see the baptism firsthand.

Some churches invite the parents and their infant to the church school classes that day to let the children see the baby and talk about what it means to be welcomed into God's family. After baptism, the pastor or an elder will sometimes walk with the infant through the sanctuary, giving every member present a chance to see the little one they've just welcomed and promised to nurture. If the children have gone to the front to observe the baptism, they might be invited to follow the elder around the sanctuary and to sit down as they come to their families.

All of these rituals and symbols help teach children—and adults—the spiritual reality that lies behind their own baptisms.

However, we must admit that the mystery of baptism eludes even adults at times. What really happens between a child and God in baptism? How do we account for baptized, covenant children who leave the faith? How has the event of baptism affected our own lives and spirituality?

The Lord's Supper also eludes our attempts to define its meaning. Who can fully understand what it means to be nurtured by Christ's body and blood?

Reformed and Presbyterian churches are taking another look at the issue of welcoming children to the Lord's Supper. Among the questions they are asking are these: If we *baptize* children into God's family without evidence of repentance or faith, should we not also include them in the sacrament of communion as a reminder to them of their membership in the communion and fellowship of God's family? What role might participation in the Lord's Supper play in nourishing our children's faith? How does a personal knowledge and an intellectual understanding of God's grace relate to receiving the bread and wine of communion? Should public profession of faith precede a welcome to the table?

It's possible that some children may treat the sacrament flippantly at times. Adults, too, can mistreat the sacraments. Paul had to reprimand the Corinthian Christians for the way they were behaving at the table. But even these disturbances give us the opportunity to teach, to model, to explain and answer questions. In the process, we learn along with the children.

If your church is seeking new ways to make the Lord's Supper meaningful to children, you will need to help the entire congregation focus on this issue. In addition to teaching children about the meaning of communion, you will need to model the attitudes and behavior befitting our participation at the table.

You might also want to look at the frequency with which you celebrate this most moving and nourishing feast. The physical feasting on the body and blood of the Word of God is to balance the weekly feasting on the spoken Word. Both offer God's grace to us, and the symbolic power and meaning of the bread and wine grows within us and our children as we experience it regularly.

Is four times a year often enough? John Calvin didn't think so.

> The Lord's Table should have been spread at least once a week for the assembly of Christians, and the promises declared in it should feed us spiritually. None is indeed to be forcibly compelled, but all are to be urged and aroused; also the inertia of indolent people is to be rebuked. All, like hungry men, should flock to such a bounteous repast.
>
> Institutes, *IV, xvii, 46*

Our adult fear that weekly communion will cause us to take the sacrament for granted misses the point. We could learn here from the children among us, who march into the house and announce with conviction, "I'm hungry!" Our week-long skirmish with the world and with our own weakness leaves us in need of nourishment, in need of the meal that proclaims God's forgiveness and love.

God has gifts in the service that are available to children, gifts that will draw them into worship. In light of our promises at baptism and in light of the ways in which our adult worship will be enriched, let's bring out these gifts in worship.

SUGGESTIONS FOR GROUP SESSION

Opening

As an opening exercise, you might have in the center of the room a table with a loaf of bread and a chalice of grape juice or wine. Distribute paper and pens and take time to sit around the table in silence for a few minutes, reflecting on the symbols that are before you. Think about the meaning of what you see and write down images, ideas, memories, Scripture passages, or prayers that come to mind.

After about five minutes, open with prayer, asking that the Lord who is present in the bread and the wine also be present in your discussion today.

Share some of the things you've written down. Explore the different ideas and images, the theological connections and the personal memories that group members have reflected on. Then talk as a group about the power of symbols to evoke many different levels of meaning and memory. Would this time of reflection have been as meaningful if it had been a five-minute lecture on God's grace? What's the difference between this kind of activity and the left-brain kinds of logic, reasoning, and analysis? How are both valuable?

For Discussion

1. What are some ways in which everyone in your congregation could bring something—a gift, a talent, an insight, a need—to your worship? Would this make worship more meaningful for you? Why or why not? How do you think the children would respond? What might it teach them about worship?
2. How does your church celebrate the sacraments of baptism and the Lord's Supper? How do they enrich your sense of worship? What special things does your church do to help children (and adults) become more aware of the meaning of these sacraments? What would you like to see happen that is not currently being done?
3. How does your congregation carry out its baptismal vows in worship? How are your children "received, prayed for, instructed, encouraged, and sustained" in the worshiping family of believers? What more might your church do?
4. Ask yourselves the same questions that were raised earlier in the session about the issue of children at the Lord's Supper. What do you see as the relationship, if any, between baptism and communion? What do you think should determine a person's readiness to be included in the Supper? Do you see the Lord's Supper as a means of nurture or as a sign that one has arrived at a proper understanding of the faith?
5. What are some ways in which children have modeled the kingdom of God for you? How might children be given the opportunity to model those qualities in worship? What changes could you make in your congregation's worship to reflect the qualities of the kingdom that children possess?
6. Change does not come easily or quickly. What changes suggested in this lesson do you feel uncomfortable with? Why? If you feel that certain changes would be good, what do you think would be the best way to implement them? What are some important things to keep in mind when disagreements arise? How should they be handled? What disagreements exist within your own study group?

Closing

To close your session you might want to use this praise selection from a small psalmist:

A Prayer of DeAna

Dear God, We know
  we have done bad things,
But we want You to forgive us.
We love You, And we know You love us,
  And that You will never leave us.
We want You to be proud of us
  and not disappointed.
We ask You to give us
  deliverance, strength, and especially
Protection from Satan, sin and lies.
You're our Father and our Creator
  And we thank You for making us.
You are the most important thing in our life
And we love You dearly.

     —from Psalms of the Dawn Treaders, *a collection of*
        psalms written by the students of Dawn Treader
        Christian School, Paterson, New Jersey.

THE WORSHIP CONNECTION

It was a lazy Sunday afternoon—the evening service just a few hours away. I didn't really want to bring it up, but a sense of duty compelled me. "What do you think, kids? Do you remember what the minister said this morning about families bringing something to the service tonight?"

"It's the fruit of the Spirit, Mom," said Rachel. "We're supposed to bring something about love."

"Love," repeated Neal. He picked up a red crayon and tried it out on the picture Rachel had been coloring.

"Cut that out!" Rachel grabbed the crayon out of his hand. "Mom, Neal's scribbling on my coloring book!" She gave him a little push.

Neal's eyes got bigger. "I'm *not* scribbling!" He pushed her back.

"Mom, Neal pushed me!" She gave him a harder shove, and he fell over, chair and all. There was a bloody lip, a lot of crying, and I yelled at them both.

Oh, how I hated times like that. One small thing would go wrong, one sharp word, one small push, and it suddenly escalated into a full-blown fight.

81

As I thought about that, something clicked in my mind. I found a piece of paper and sat down at the table. "See, kids, here's a heavy brick." I drew a small rectangle and colored it in with a dark crayon. "This is something we do or say to make someone else feel bad."

I drew another brick underneath it, this time twice as large. "And this is what the other person does back when they're angry, and the bad feelings just get bigger."

I drew a final brick, bigger than the others, at the bottom of the page. "And this is what happens at the end, when people keep doing worse and worse things to each other. It's just a big, bad feeling."

Then I took another sheet of paper and drew a small red heart at the top. "This is just a little something—maybe saying something nice to somebody or sharing something with them."

I drew a bigger heart underneath it. "Here's what the other person does or says back, because they feel so good about what the first person said. See, it gets bigger now."

The final red heart at the bottom was huge. "And this is how everyone ends up feeling. It just keeps growing and growing and growing."

Rachel looked at the shapes. "I get it. It's about love and hate. Hey, Mom, we could bring this to church tonight," she said. Hmmm—just what I was thinking.

From our shapes we made two mobiles—and a third one to show what happens when someone starts out hateful, but the other person responds with love:

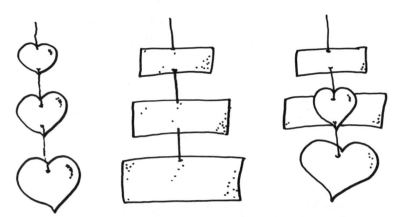

That evening when it was our family's turn, we stood up together and explained our mobiles. The simplicity and meaning of the shapes seemed to catch people's eyes, especially the children's. The minister asked us to hang our creation at the front of church, where everyone could see it in the coming weeks. He referred to it several times in his sermons, and others responded to it during our regular sharing times.

This incident may seem rather small and insignificant. It does, however, point out how the worship activities of the family and the larger church community can connect and enrich each other.

If our minister had not encouraged each family to bring something to the evening service, I wouldn't have been alert to the teaching possibilities in the situation that Sunday afternoon. And had not we—and other families—brought our insights and stories to the service that night, our worship together for the next several weeks would not have been enriched by the variety of ways God's Word was shared through each of us.

If God intends the home to be the primary place where children learn to know and worship him, then the flow between church and home—in ideas, in atmosphere, in teaching—should be lively. Worship in church should stimulate worship in the home, and vice versa.

If the flow is only a trickle, churches may find their worship stale and dull, lacking in fresh ideas and spontaneity. Families will find church a place where they come to do something, not bring something. And they will bring little back with them for their own life and worship. Church and family worship will be unconnected.

Decades ago, when churches were often located in small, close-knit ethnic communities, this kind of vital interchange between church and home didn't seem as necessary. Families knew what went on in each other's lives; they lived, shopped, visited, celebrated, and gossiped together. Worship was just one more place to gather among a faith community where they were already closely connected.

Today, however, many families move every five or ten years. There is greater ethnic diversity in the church, along with a growing emphasis on attracting people from different backgrounds. As a result, families feel the need for more "connected" worship. Churches need to serve as an extended family where parents and children can bring their insights, concerns, and gifts to worship—and bring home stories of faith to talk about, new ideas for discussion, and creative ways to enrich their family worship.

How the Church Can Strengthen Family Worship

Education

Education is one area in which the church is already well-equipped to strengthen family worship. Classes, teachers, and fellowship groups are in place in most congregations.

As the previous session mentioned, educating children about worship is vital to their enjoyment and participation in corporate worship. But the church can go a step beyond that. It can provide teaching times in which parents and young children learn about worship together and bring their new knowledge and experiences home to talk about and work on as a family.

In their helpful book, *Children in the Worshiping Community*, David Ng and Virginia Thomas provide a model for a course for parents and children (first and second graders) on the meaning of congregational worship. The authors suggest some excellent, creative ways to educate families about worship. Churches that wish to develop their own course for parents and children could look at Ng and Thomas's suggestions (see *Children in the Worshiping Community*, chapter 5) and adapt these for their own situations.

Participation

In addition to educating, however, churches should also suggest ways to connect family and congregational worship—and actively encourage families to do so.

The following are some suggestions for integrating home and church worship, things that might stimulate families to carry over the focus of the congregational worship into their own homes. Again, use these as a springboard for your own ideas. Remember that what works in one church may fall flat in another, depending on the size of the church, the expectations of its members, and the degree of fellowship among members.

The evening service may be a good place to start, since it's traditionally less formal than the morning service. Generally, fewer people attend this service, which makes for a more intimate atmosphere. Sharing family insights or experiences may come easier. And using a different format may provide a welcome change from the more structured liturgy of the morning.

For example, you might schedule a series on the fruits of the Spirit. Offer families suggestions for carrying out specific themes during the coming week. Here's a sampler of suggestions that focus on *patience*:

• Keep a record of each situation this week in your home that requires patience (e.g., Dad took too long in the shower, the baby was teething and fussy, James still hasn't heard whether he made the soccer team, Jill spent 45 minutes on the phone, Mom was late in picking up the kids from school). Post a chart on the refrigerator to keep track of your responses. On a scale of 1 to 10, how much patience did each of you show in these situations?

During mealtime or devotions, talk about your "patience prodders"; laugh over them, pray about them. At the end of the week review your record. Remember, this is not a time to point fingers but to laugh together about your difficult times and talk about the things that require patience. Don't focus on the person who was to blame for the situation; focus instead on your response. How do you think Jesus would have responded in your situation?

• In your family devotions, read Jesus' parable of the servant who begged for the king's patience (Matthew 18:23–35). If you have enough people, act it out (and have fun with all the ways you can express the emotions in this passage). Read also Paul's advice on how to live together as a family (Colossians 3:12–15). What do these Bible passages tell us about patience? What does patience have to do with forgiving each other? Why is forgiveness important in a family? When did you ever need someone to be patient with you? How did it feel when they were patient/impatient with you?

• If you have a concordance (a book that lists all the places that certain words appear in the Bible), look up the words *patient*, *patience*, and *patiently*. Read them together as a family, then answer these questions: How many of these verses refer to God? In what kinds of situations was God patient? Would you have been that patient? In what kinds of situations today might God be patient with you?

The following Sunday evening, provide time for individuals or families to share what they've learned about patience during the week.

Informal discussion like this may be a big change for your church. Any change comes slowly. Don't expect everyone to participate at first; members will need time to get used to the idea, to "wait and see" what others will do. If your church is very large, you may want to do this kind of sharing in weekly fellowship groups instead, or break your evening worship service up into smaller groups for the time of sharing.

Another way to encourage families to work with worship themes at home is to set up a table in a conspicuous place in the narthex or the back of the sanctuary. Ask families to bring in things they've made or done in response to the sermons and teachings of the week before. Children might bring in a picture they colored, depicting the Bible story or some concept from the sermon (children love to display their art work). Families might make a mobile, put together a collage of magazine pictures, write a poem, or make a banner or piece of art work to express their response to the congregational worship. If they've done a special project during the week, they might write up a report of what they've done. Encourage people to be as expressive as their creativity leads them to be.

The pastor might mention one or two of these family projects each week in the sermon, reminding the congregation to browse at the table after the service—and to come with their own responses. Church education teachers can also encourage the children in their classes to bring something for the "family table."

Related to this idea of a "family table" is the suggestion that parents have their children listen for things in the sermon that will spark ideas for drawings, projects, or books to read. When the family gets home from church, everyone should have at least one idea to share.

You could also print the schedule of Scripture readings to be used in worship for the month ahead. (For those churches using the lectionary this would be especially easy to do.) Encourage families to read the appropriate Scripture the week ahead so that they're "primed" for the sermon topic, or recommend that they read it during the week following the sermon to refresh their memory of the teaching and follow it up with discussion. Either way, this repetition will be invaluable; children need repetition in order for new ideas and words to sink in.

You might want to set up a bulletin board in church on which you post the names or pictures of all the members who are celebrating birthdays or anniversaries that week. Pray for each person specifically during the service, and encourage members to pray for these people during their family prayers as well. This is an excellent way to remember to pray for all the members of your church throughout the year. (It's also very affirming to the people having birthdays and anniversaries!)

If your church uses a pitcher of wine, a chalice, and a loaf of bread for its communion service, consider asking one of your church families to carry the bread and the wine in before the communion liturgy begins.

Some churches begin the service by carrying a cross and the Bible down the aisle to the front of the sanctuary as visual reminders of God's presence and Word in worship. As with the elements of communion, families can take turns carrying the cross and the Bible down the aisle each week. Children will enjoy the movement and symbolism of this ritual and will also anticipate their own family's turn in coming weeks.

Using the Liturgical Year

The celebration of seasons and holy days provides a natural rhythm in the church's life. There are two major cycles in the Christian year: the Christmas cycle and the Easter cycle. Each begins with a time of spiritual preparation (Advent and Lent), and follows the celebration of Christ's birth and resurrection with a time for reflection and growth (Epiphany and the time after Pentecost) as the good news of salvation is proclaimed throughout the world. The themes of waiting, repentance, love, joy, peace, prophecy, celebration, passion, and sorrow are all woven into the church year, helping to focus the worship of families and congregations.

Celebrating the liturgical year is also a very visual way of remembering these major events. Many symbols are associated with the seasonal celebrations: candles, palm branches, stars, butterflies, wreaths, crowns, mangers, vines, flames of fire, and so on. Moreover, each season and holy day is commemorated with a color that helps us remember the meaning of that day or period. The deep purple color of Lent and Advent (some churches use blue for Advent), for example, symbolizes the time of waiting, of introspection and preparation, the time of getting ready for the coming Messiah.

Because the church year is rich in visual imagery, symbols, and color, it offers many teaching opportunities as well as providing a natural link between church and family worship. A closer look at each season will provide a variety of suggestions for integrating the worship times of home and congregation.

The Christmas Cycle: Advent, Christmas, Epiphany

The Advent wreath is perhaps one of the most familiar visuals that help prepare us for the celebration of Jesus' birth. Each candle represents one of the four weeks before Christmas. The first four candles are purple, the fifth is white. (In some wreaths the third candle, the candle of joy, is pink.)

The four Advent candles stand in a circle around the Christ candle, placed on a wreath. The circle of the wreath symbolizes our eternal God and His continual presence throughout human history. The evergreen branches of the wreath remind us of the eternal life offered in Christ.

Each Sunday in Advent, the church lights another candle in the Advent wreath and listens to the explanation of its symbolism. This is an excellent place to include families in the candle lighting, in the explanation of the symbols, and in the reading of the Scriptures and litanies for each week. The church can also provide Scripture readings and family litanies in printed form for families to take home and use with their own Advent wreaths.

The Advent wreath is a meaningful family ritual as well—one that children greet with anticipation and excitement. It has become an indispensable part of our family's Advent devotions. The Scripture readings and litany serve to draw the children's focus away from the materialism of our culture's Christmas celebration and back to the hope and joy that are found in the newborn Babe. The symbolism of the light and the chance to participate in the liturgy are what attract the children to this ritual.

There are other ways to integrate church and family worship during Christmas and Advent. Some churches use the Christmas Eve service to celebrate the ways in which their members are gifts to each other. This evening service is set aside for individuals and families to share their talents through singing, drama, poetry, instrumental music—a celebration of the gifts God has given to the church not only through Christ but also through his children.

During the celebration of Christmas, the church can also encourage families to participate in activities that help teach the spirit of giving: gathering gifts of money and presents for those who can't afford food or clothing, making gifts for each other that say something special, responding to the needs of refugees and disaster victims, sending cards and gifts to missionaries and overseas workers, making family Advent banners, opening your home to people who are alone over the holidays, and so on. *Alternatives*, an organization working in cooperation with the Reformed Church in America, has produced a helpful booklet entitled "Whose Birthday Is It, Anyway?" (available from RCA Distribution Center, 3000 Ivanrest SW, Grandville, MI 49418). Through these activities, children learn that worship is not only expressed in song, dance, prayer, and quiet reflection, but also in offering ourselves and our belongings to God.

The celebration of Christmas traditionally lasts twelve days, until January 6. The colors of Christmas are white and gold, symbolizing gladness, light, and joy. Epiphany Day, January 6, is a time to remember the adoration of the wise men. Epiphany celebrates Christ's coming to the Gentiles; it's a joyous remembrance that we too are now included in the people of God. Because of its meaning, it's particularly appropriate that the Gentile church keep this day. The color of Epiphany Day is primarily white, in a continuation of the celebration of Christmas, but gold is also used, symbolizing the gifts of the Magi.

In many countries, the feasting and exchange of gifts takes place on this day, rather than on Christmas, in commemoration of the gifts the Magi presented to Jesus. At Christmas we celebrate God's gift to us in Christ; at Epiphany we focus on the gift of worship we give back to God.

Churches can help families focus on Epiphany by suggesting activities like these:

- With your family, use the twelve days between Christmas and Epiphany to think of a gift your family can offer to Jesus, just as the wise men did at Bethlehem. It can be anything: a picture, a poem or other writing, an act of service to someone in the community, a song, a gift to missions or to your denomination's relief agencies.

  Then gather as a church family to celebrate Twelfth Night, the eve of Epiphany, with a potluck supper and a night of games. Enjoy the drama of the story of the wise men, and offer your family "gifts."

- For your family devotions in the days before Epiphany, draw (or cut out) pictures that represent the things in our lives that we can give to Christ as gifts of worship, just as the Magi did. Bring your "gifts" to church the Sunday following Epiphany and add them to a wall mural displayed in the sanctuary. Be creative, and encourage children especially to contribute their art work!

During the season of Epiphany we learn more about Christ's ministry on earth and how he was revealed as the Savior for the whole world. The color of Epiphany season is green, symbolizing a time to grow in understanding who Christ is and what he did while he was on earth.

The Easter Cycle: Lent, Easter, Pentecost

Lent, with its beginnings in the first centuries of Christianity, was initially a time of prayerful scrutiny for those who wanted to embrace the Christian faith. Before converts were baptized on Easter Sunday, the traditional day for baptisms in the early church, they spent time in intense prayer and reflection on the Christian life. By the fifth century, Lent had become a time for all Christians to look inward, to repent of sins, and to seek forgiveness in the name of the crucified Christ. Today, Lent remains a time when believers everywhere prepare for the celebration of Christ's death and resurrection.

Sin, repentance, and forgiveness are themes that older children can reflect on and understand, along with the adults. Young children, however, don't have a sense of moral conscience that makes them aware of guilt and sin within themselves. They know they displease Mom and Dad sometimes, but young children aren't able to reflect on these themes along with the rest of the congregation during the season of Lent.

Sofia Cavelletti suggests using the story of the good shepherd during Lent to help children focus on the One who was willing to lay down his life for his sheep. Of all the parables that Jesus told, this one seems to appeal most to children. The figure of the good shepherd comforts them and calms their fears. It teaches them to trust a God of tender love who guides and cares for them. As they grow older, they will learn that the good shepherd gave his life for their sins as well. But for now it is enough for them to know of his love.

Churches can help families make Lent a time of quiet and reflection in the home:

• Provide families with "family journals" to use during Lent. (Stapling together twenty 8½" x 10" plain sheets inside a construction-paper cover makes a simple booklet containing a page for each of the forty days of Lent.)

Also provide a list of Scriptures that focus on Lenten sermon themes. After the family has read a Scripture passage together, ask individuals to take fifteen minutes to be alone and to write or draw in their journals a response to what they have read and discussed. (Parents can simply ask younger children to draw a picture-message for God of something that happened during the day.)

• During Holy Week (the week before Easter), ask families to use part of their devotional time at home to talk about ways in which they need God's forgiveness as a family—for lack of communication, being too busy for each other, not sharing enough in chores or family duties, arguing, withholding forgiveness from each other, and so on. (Ask singles or those not living with immediate family to reflect on their relationship to their long-distance families.) Write down all the areas in which you need God's forgiveness and healing; then use your prayer time to bring these areas of your family life to God and to ask for his healing.

On Good Friday (or Maundy Thursday, if your church prefers to meet on that night), ask everyone to bring that list to the service. After a time of reflecting on Christ's suffering and death, collect the papers in a basket. Offer a prayer for forgiveness and grace through Christ's death on the cross. Emphasize that these visual reminders of our sins are now to be forgotten. (You might shred the papers in front of the congregation as a graphic demonstration symbolizing the complete forgiveness that comes through Christ's blood.)

• For young children, study the parable of the good shepherd in church education during Lent (unless the pastor plans to share this story during Lent with children and adults in the congregational worship). Use both visual and theatrical methods of presenting the story. The book *Young Children and Worship* by Jerome

Berryman and Sonja Stewart (Westminster Press, 1990) provides a simple retelling of the parable and patterns for the visuals, along with suggestions for telling the story effectively to children.

For an art response, help the children cut out figures of the good shepherd and the sheep, along with a sheepfold and a pool of water, to retell the story at home. Ask the parents to work on the parable with their children during Lent, and provide a list of suggestions for doing so.

There are a wealth of opportunities for integrating family and corporate worship during Lent and Easter, using the many symbols that point back to the history and meaning of Christ's death and resurrection. Here are a few:

• Make a banner of Lenten and Easter symbols, designed by different families at home (bread and wine, crown of thorns, cross, butterfly, lilies, palm branches—even hot cross buns and pretzels!). Ask each family to research the history and meaning of their symbol and explain it to the congregation. As for Advent and Christmas, the colors for Lent and Easter are gold, white, and purple.
• Distribute palm branches on Palm Sunday to wave as part of your celebration of Jesus' triumphal entry into Jerusalem. Encourage families to take the palm branches home and use them for a family praise time, in which members think of reasons to praise God, corresponding with each separate leaf of the palm branch.
• Give families information on how to have a Seder meal (Jewish Passover meal) to commemorate Jesus' supper with his disciples on Maundy Thursday and to remember how the Passover event looked forward to the death of the Lamb of God.
• Tie family activities and devotions in to an Ash Wednesday service.
• Plan for families' creative involvement in an Easter vigil service on Saturday evening.
• Encourage church families to gather for festive dinners during Eastertide (the fifty days between Easter and Pentecost), in contrast to the more solemn and introspective mood of Lent.

However you choose to connect your congregational and home worship during the season of Lent, emphasize the joy and glory of Easter and the love of the good shepherd, who lays down his life for the sheep.

Pentecost Sunday, a "week of weeks" after Easter, marks the outpouring of God's Spirit on the infant church and on the generations of believers that have followed. The six months that follow Pentecost are known as "ordinary time," since this time contains no feast days or preparations for major holy days. Instead of focusing on events in Christ's life, the season of Pentecost looks toward the work of the Spirit and the journey of the Christian life.

Pentecost itself should be a feast of color and light. Red, the liturgical color of that day, should be prominent everywhere—from table napkins at the breakfast and dinner table to the banners and table runners in the church. What better opportunity to stimulate children's questions and to explain the kind of power the Holy Spirit brings to our lives?

For the last several years our church asked its members to wear something red to the worship service on Pentecost. Entire families have come dressed in bright red; our services have been alive with color. We've emphasized that people can feel free to wear clothing that isn't generally considered church "style": red sneakers, T-shirts, scarves, and so on. Young and old alike enjoy participating in this different sort of pageantry. And homes are filled with questions on Pentecost morning when it's time to get ready for church: "Why are we wearing red today?" "What does red have to do with Pentecost?"

During the six months of ordinary time, congregations may want to provide their families with devotional materials that emphasize spiritual growth and the development of the Holy Spirit's gifts in each member of the family. Some of the activities mentioned above can also be adapted to fit this theme. The color for this portion of the church year is green, symbolizing our growth in the Christian faith.

General Suggestions for the Church Year

In keeping with the changing colors of the liturgical seasons, many churches change colors in the sanctuary: table runners, cloth pulpit hangings, banners, communion napkins, liturgical stoles for the pastor. To bring this to the children's attention, consider making the changes during the service itself, when the children can watch. Ask some of the children to bring one item at a time away from the front of the sanctuary and replace it with an item of the new color. The pastor and worship leader can also take off their stoles and ask the children to bring replacements of the new color. These situations offer an excellent opportunity to explain again the meaning of the new liturgical season and the symbolism of the colors and signs.

Families can carry this theme over into their own worship by adding liturgical color to their homes as well. Table runners, candles, tablecloths, napkins, banners, even the bookmark for the Bible stories—these are visuals that speak without words to the children about the rhythm of the church year.

If you have set up a private area for prayer in your home, you may want to include there a small table for the children, on which you place a cloth of the appropriate liturgical color and a collection of children's books, art reproductions, and other symbols that speak of the meaning of the season or holy day that is approaching. Young children will enjoy coming to this place and exploring the things you've set out. This also provides an excellent discussion starter on the major themes of your worship.

Connecting church and family worship is not always easy. But it can make worship come alive. Far more possibilities exist than appear in this lesson. Many have not been thought of or tried yet—and that's where your own creativity comes in. Don't be afraid to explore the symbols that teach us about the mystery of God and of our faith. Let God's Spirit show you new ways to worship and experience God together.

SUGGESTIONS FOR GROUP SESSION

Opening

Read together the challenge of the last paragraph. Then read an opening psalm of praise. (Check Psalm 145–150.)

For Discussion

1. Think back on your family devotions as you were growing up or as you've been raising your own children. At what time, if any, did the church's worship on Sunday influence or stimulate your worship at home? When did family worship help the children become more interested and enthusiastic about the worship service with the congregation?

   Building on these experiences, work together as a group to come up with two or three suggestions for your church to integrate its corporate worship with the family devotional times of its members.
2. Divide into small groups of two to four members each. Assign each group a part of the service (call to worship, prayer of confession, congregational prayer, hymn singing, sermon, offertory, and so on) and ask each group to pick a liturgical season or holy day to work with. Each group member is to come up with one suggestion for linking this part of the service to its respective liturgical year and/or involving families in the service at this point.

   Share ideas from the small groups with the larger group. Could any of these suggestions be adapted for family worship? Would any of these suggestions work with your congregation? Why or why not?

3. What did you think of the suggestions for family worship presented in this lesson? Might they serve to lead your family into
   worship? What other ideas came to your mind as you read
   through the lesson?
4. Distribute pencils and paper. Take a few minutes for everyone to
   write down any benefits that might come from observing the
   "preparation times" of Advent and Lent. How might these times of
   preparation be related to the actual celebration of Christmas and
   Easter?

   After writing down your responses, discuss them together.
   What things in our culture and lifestyle might make such a time
   of preparation necessary? What is the value of remembering
   and preparing? How would you like to see this done in your
   own church?

Closing

You might want to close this session—and end this course—with
voluntary sentence prayers, inviting group members to pray as the
Spirit moves them for congregational and family worship that includes and invites every member to worship God fully and joyfully!

RESOURCES

Celebrating the Church Year with Young Children by Joan Halmo (Liturgical Press, 1988).

Advent: A Congregational Life/Intergenerational Experience by Trudy Vander Haar (RCA Office for Education).

To Celebrate: Reshaping Holidays & Rites of Passage (Alternatives Organization, 1989, available from the RCA Office for Education).

Christ In Christmas: A Family Advent Celebration by James Dobson, Charles Swindoll, James Montgomery Boyce and R. C. Sproul (Navpress: Colorado Springs CO. 1989).

Another helpful resource is *Reformed Worship*, a quarterly magazine (available from CRC Publications) that provides many creative ideas for planning worship services. Each September issue has resources for Advent, Christmas, and Epiphany; the December issue covers Lent and Easter; the March issue deals with Ascension and Pentecost; and each June issue provides ideas for fall worship service planning.